NEW TOWNS
IN
INDIA

VED PRAKASH

NEW TOWNS
IN
INDIA

VED PRAKASH

DUKE UNIVERSITY
Program in Comparative Studies on Southern Asia

MONOGRAPH AND OCCASIONAL PAPERS SERIES

Monograph Number Eight

EXCLUSIVE DISTRIBUTORS:
THE CELLAR BOOK SHOP
18090 WYOMING
DETROIT, MICH. 48221
U.S.A.

PREFACE AND ACKNOWLEDGEMENTS

This monograph is based upon research and field work conducted in India during 1963-64. The author spent a period of one to two weeks at each of the seventeen new towns selected for detailed investigation pertaining to their planning procedures and standards, the costs of development, and methods of financing (see questionnaire in Appendix A). These seventeen towns are located in nine states, and they include two refugee towns, two state capitals, two towns sponsored by the States of Mysore and West Bengal respectively, one town developed in conjunction with a multipurpose irrigation and hydroelectric project, four steel towns, one fertilizer town, one new town sponsored by the Heavy Engineering Corporation, and four other industrial towns.

The author wishes to acknowledge his indebtedness to several people who reviewed all or portions of the manuscript and offered many valuable suggestions. Prominent among them were Professors Arch Dotson, A. M. Hillhouse, Barclay G. Jones, Cornell University; Professors Marshall B. Clinard and Leo Jakobson, University of Wisconsin; Dr. John J. Carroll, previously a member of the Ford Foundation Advisory team, Calcutta Metropolitan Plan Project and now with the Social Security Administration, U. S. Department of Health, Education, and Welfare; Professor Britton Harris, Institute for Environmental Studies, University of Pennsylvania; Professor Wallace Reed, Duke University; J. P. Sah, Town and Country Planning Organization, Government of India; and Lowdon Wingo, Jr., Resources for the Future, Inc.

The study was made possible by a Ford Foundation fellowship and travel grant during 1963-65 and the author owes a special debt of gratitude to them. A research grant for the preparation of the manuscript was provided by the Graduate School of the University of Wisconsin during the summer of 1966.

In addition, the author acknowledges with gratitude the help and cooperation provided by the various agencies in India responsible for the planning and development of new towns, as well as different ministries and departments of the Central Government and the several State Governments.

Ved Prakash
December 1968
University of Wisconsin
Madison, Wisconsin

TABLE OF CONTENTS

Page

LIST OF TABLES

Table

LIST OF FIGURES

CHAPTER I

INDIA'S NEW TOWNS

Since independence in 1947, more than thirty new towns
have been planned and built in India. Immediately after independence, as expressions of regional pride, new state capitals for
Punjab and Orissa were begun at Chandigarh and Bhubneshwar
respectively, and towns to rehabilitate refugees from Pakistan
were established. With the launching of India's First Five Year
Plan in 1951, a number of towns were built in conjunction with
new dams and irrigation and power projects. In succeeding plan
periods, heavy emphasis was placed on the establishment of
major industries in public ownership resulting in the planning
and development of several new industrial towns.

Generally these new towns have been designed for a size
and functional range opposite to the current trend of Indian urbanization. In view of the cost of development and the limited
impact of new towns on India's urbanization process, planning
practitioners have expressed strong concern with both the policies for establishing such towns and with the standards set for
their development. [1]

In this study the role of these new towns is examined within
the context of economic development and the urbanization policies

---

[1] Leo Jakobson, "Regional Planning for Urbanization in
Eastern India, " Improvement Programme for Metropolitan Calcutta: 1964-1971, Report No. 21b (Calcutta: Calcutta Metropolitan Planning Organization, 1965); S. Saeedush Shafi, "New Towns
the Answer to Urban Congestion--Future Pattern of Growth for
Communities, " The Statesman (Calcutta: September 22, 1964),
p. 6; J. P. Sah and S. S. Dutta, "Economic Development and
Spatial Planning in India, " Ekistics, Vol. 23, No. 134 (January,
1967), pp. 33-39; L. R. Vagle, Population Trends in India and
Their Implications in Town Planning, Housing and Urban Development (a paper presented to the Asian Population Conference,
New Delhi, December, 1963).

outlined in India's Five Year Plans. Of particular interest are the nature, principles, and concepts utilized in the planning of such communities, the capital, maintenance and operating costs for various urban facilities (including housing), and the methods of financing these costs.   In the light of this examination several proposals for improving the cost structure in development of India's new towns are put forward.

India's Recent Urbanization

The population of India in 1900 was 236 million (Table 1). By 1961 it had risen to 439 million and by 1976 may reach 625 million.[2] While the urban population in 1921 was about 29 million and constituted a little over 11 per cent of the total, by 1961 the population in urban areas had reached 78 million and accounted for 19 per cent of the total population.   If, as the Planning Commission has assumed, a 4 per cent rate of growth for the urban population continues during the 1961-76 period, India's urban population may grow from 78 to 140 million by 1976, with an expected 25 per cent of the total population living in urban centers.[3]

A careful study of the urbanization process from 1951 to 1961 is useful.   In this decade both development within a planning context and the construction of most of the new towns were initiated.   The growth in urban population during 1951-61 seemed

---

[2] India (Republic), Planning Commission, The Third Five Year Plan (New Delhi: Government of India Press, 1961), p. 751. (Cited hereafter as The Third Five Year Plan.)

[3] The National Council of Applied Economic Research in Population Projections of India 1961-1976 (New Delhi, 1960), projected the growth rate for urban population at 5.2 per cent per annum, consisting of 2.3 per cent for natural increase and 2.9 per cent for rural-to-urban migration. At this rate the urban population in 1976 would be somewhat higher than 140 million.   In a 1962 study, Long Term Projections of Demand for and Supply of Selected Agricultural Commodities 1960-61 to 1975-76, the National Council of Applied Economic Research projected the urban population at 93 million in 1966 and 108 million in 1971--an average annual arithmetic growth rate of 3.25 per cent.

TABLE 1

Urbanization in India: 1901-1961

Census Year	Total Population (in Millions)	Per Cent Variation Per Decade	Urban Population (in Millions)	Per Cent Variation Per Decade	Per Cent Urban of Total Population
1901	236.3	--	25.7	--	10.9
1911	252.1	+ 5.73	26.6	+ 2.4	10.6
1921	251.4	- 0.3	28.6	+ 7.3	11.4
1931	279.0	+11.0	33.8	+18.4	12.1
1941	318.7	+14.2	44.3	+31.1	13.9
1951	361.1	+13.3	62.6	+41.2	17.3
1961	439.2	+21.5	78.8	+25.9	19.0

Source: Census of India, Paper No. 1 of 1962, Final Population Totals (New Delhi: Government of of India Press, 1962).

lower than the growth during the preceding two decades and led some observers to suggest that India's urbanization process had slackened. However, while changes in the Census definition of urban population were marginal from 1901 to 1951, they were quite significant between the 1951 and 1961 Censuses.[4] When the 1961 Census definition is applied, the urban population in 1951 becomes 54 million rather than the 63 million reported in the 1951 Census,[5] and the urban population increases by 25 million or 45 per cent during this decade. Thus, the urbanization process probably has accelerated rather than slowed down.

The distribution of population according to six city-size categories of the Indian Census for 1951 and for 1961 is shown in Table 2. About 24 million persons, or 38 per cent of the total urban population, lived in 74 cities of over 100,000 each in 1951. By 1961, there were 107 such cities with 35 million residents or 44.5 per cent of the total urban population in that year. The relative population share of the three larger categories of urban areas increased while the share of the smaller towns declined.

Table 3 shows the relative growth of population in different sized urban areas. The classification used here subdivides the first census category (100,000 and over) into three categories and groups together the urban areas under 50,000 (Census categories III through VI). The cities with a population of 500,000 to 999,999 show the highest rate of growth, 66 per cent. Smaller cities and towns as well as the million plus metropolis cities experience

---

[4] Ashish Bose, "A Note on the Definition of 'Town' in the Indian Censuses 1901-61," Indian Economic and Social History Review, Vol. 1, No. 3 (January-March, 1964), pp. 1-11. The definition of a town varied from one state to another up to the 1951 Census. In 1961, the Census first attempted to use a uniform and vigorous standard for enumerating urban areas. Along with areas that had some form of urban local government, areas meeting with three other criteria were also considered urban: (1) a population of not less than 5,000; (2) a density of not less than 1,000 persons per square mile; and (3) at least three-fourths of the adult male population in non-agricultural pursuits.

[5] M. K. Premi, "Reclassification of the 1951 Census Population into Rural and Urban Areas on the Basis of 1961 Census Population or Urban Areas, Indian Population Bulletin No. 11 (New Delhi: Government of India Press, 1961), p. 320.

4

TABLE 2

Population of Urban Areas in 1951 and 1961 According to Size of Towns

Class and Size	Number of Urban Areas		Population in '000			
			1951		1961	
	1951	1961	Population	Percentage of Total	Population	Percentage of Total
I 100,000 and over	74	107	23,725	38.1	35,110	44.5
II 50,000 to 99,999	111	141	7,545	12.1	9,626	12.2
III 20,000 to 49,999	375	515	11,135	17.9	15,650	19.9
IV 10,000 to 19,999	670	817	9,291	14.9	11,258	14.3
V 5,000 to 9,999	1,189	844	8,472	13.6	6,313	8.0
VI Below 5,000	638	266	2,109	3.4	879	1.1-
Total	3,057	2,690	62,277	100.0	78,836	100.0

Source: Census of India, Paper No. 1 of 1962, Final Population Totals, (New Delhi: Government of India Press, 1962), p. xxxv.

TABLE 3

Growth of Population in Different Sizes of Urban Areas: 1951-1961[a]

Per Cent Increase – 1951-1961

State	Metropolises 1,000,000 and above	Large Cities 500,000 to 999,999	Medium-Sized Cities 100,000 to 499,999	Large Towns 50,000 to 99,999	Small Towns Below 50,000	All Towns and Cities
All India (Excluding Jammu and Kashmir State and Pondicherry)	26	66	29	24	25	28
Andhra	3	-	40	44	25	25
Assam	-	-	-	35	58	55
Bihar	-	-	27	26	41	34
Gujarat	-	46	37	22	22	30
Kerala	-	-	24	30	36	31
Madhya Pradesh	-	-	34	34	35	34
Madras	22	-	21	19	14	18
Maharashtra	46	-	40	29	15	32
Mysore	-	40	30	3	21	24
Orissa	-	-	43	23	36	36
Punjab	-	-	30	20	32	29
Rajasthan	-	-	29	36	23	26
Uttar Pradesh	-	41	31	17	23	26
West Bengal	15	-	6	40	42	25
Union Territories and Other Areas	-	125	-5	n.a.	20	67

n.a. - not available.

[a] In order to make the population at the time of the two censuses comparable, the following adjustments have been made in the data of 1951 and 1961 censuses: (1) The 1961 population has been arranged according to the categories of urban areas in 1951. (2) New urban areas reported for the first time in 1961 have been excluded from the 1961 population. (3) Certain areas treated as urban in 1951 were excluded in the 1961 census from the list of urban areas. The population of such areas has been deducted from 1951 figures.

Source: Compiled from Census of India, Paper No. 1 of 1962, Final Population Totals, (New Delhi: Government of India Press, 1962), pp. xlii-lv.

only a 24-29 per cent of growth.[6] It is generally believed that between one-third and one-half of the increase in urban population from 1951 to 1961 was due to rural-to-urban migration.[7] The higher rates of growth in larger cities (population of 100,000 and over) mainly mirrors the relative scale of migration to these areas vis-a-vis smaller urban centers, and is apparently due to greater opportunities for employment found in larger cities.

The Role of Cities in the Indian Economy

This wide discrepancy in employment opportunities between larger and smaller urban areas is related to the range of functions these areas perform. Even the little that has been published on occupational structure has led a number of observers to comment on the lack of industrial and commercial diversification to be found in most Indian cities.[8] This diversification declines rapidly with decreasing city size. Industrial activity is frequently not the primary urban specialization. India's urban

---

[6]For a detailed discussion highlighting the role of the largest cities in the urbanization process, see Leo Jakobson and Ved Prakash, "Urbanization and Regional Planning." Urban Affairs Quarterly, Vol. II, No. 3 (March, 1967), pp. 41-45.

[7]Ashish Bose in "Urbanization in the Face of Rapid Population Growth and Surplus Labour--The Case of India" (A Paper submitted to the Asian Population Conference, New Delhi, December, 1963), p. 6, estimated that migration accounted for about 50 per cent of the increase in urban population. N. V. Sovani, however, suggests that the volume of migration was 5.2 million or about a third of the total increase in urban population during 1951-61. See N. V. Sovani, Urbanization and Urban India (New York: Asia Publishing House, 1966), p. 143.

[8]Britton Harris, "Urban Centralization and Planned Development," in Roy Turner (ed.), India's Urban Future (Bombay: Oxford University Press, 1962), p. 266; Tarlok Singh, "Problems of Integrating Rural, Industrial, and Urban Development," in Roy Turner (ed.), Ibid., p. 331; Ashok Mitra (A Functional Classification of India's Towns" (A Paper submitted to the All-India Seminar on Population, March, 1964); and J. P. Sah and S. S. Dutta, op. cit., pp. 35-36.

areas are generally characterized by a low proportion of manufacturing employment and a large proportion of service or tertiary employment.   Many workers in this group are self-em-
ployed petty shop-keepers such as vendors and rickshaw pullers
who make small contributions to the growth of urban economics.

Even though this is not an optimum occupational structure
for urban economic, growth, urban per capita income in 1960 was
approximately 70 per cent higher than rural per capita income
This urban per capita income is highly correlated with the size
of the city and is shown to vary considerably among specific
urban areas.   Thus economic diversification related to size has
considerable impact on the income producing abilities of India's
urban areas, the smaller places with less diversified economic
opportunities tending to have the lower per capita incomes.

This lack of adequate balance in industrial and commercial
activities results in not only an inadequate per capita income base
but also in an inadequate revenue base for smaller urban areas.
The consequent lack of municipal facilities and the inability to
finance improvements make it difficult for most smaller cities to
attract new economic activity.

Urbanization Policy and the Role of New Towns

The intention of the national and state governments to encourage development in smaller-sized cities is shown by the
number of new towns which have been built since 1947, those now
under construction (Appendix B), and the size and employment
structure for which they have been designed.

A major objective of the Five Year Plans has been a balanced regional development in India by encouraging balanced
growth among large-, medium-, and small-scale industries, and
between rural and urban areas.   In operational terms this policy
requires "extension of benefits of economic progress to less developed regions and widespread diffusion of industry."[9]   The industrial dispersal policy in turn implies that distressed or back-
ward areas should have higher claims on investment in infra-

---

[9] The Third Five Year Plan, p. 48.

8

structure to promote industrial development and employment opportunities in these regions. The Third Plan explicitly expressed the developmental policy in the following terms:

> 1. As far as possible new industries should be established away from large and congested cities.
>
> 2. In the planning of large industries, the concept of regions should be adopted. In each case, planning should extend beyond the immediate environs to a larger area for whose development new industry would serve as a major focal point.
>
> 3. In community development projects or other areas within a district, the rural and urban components of development should be knit into a composite plan based in each case on schemes for strengthening interdependence between towns and the surrounding rural areas.
>
> 4. Within each rural area the effort should be to secure a diversified occupational pattern in place of the present extreme dependence on agriculture. [10]

This dispersal of industrial activities is to be made possible through positive locational decisions for public sector industrial projects. The expansion and location of private sector industries is regulated by the Ministry of Commerce and Industry, Government of India, under the Industries (Development and Regulation) Act of 1951. While it recognizes that economic and technical considerations should largely govern the location and development of large-scale industries, [11] it, however, points out that:

> The disadvantages which particular areas may have for the location of the larger projects are not always basic or irremediable, for, at times, they may reflect only the lack of basic facilities and services. In the location of public sector projects, the claims of relatively backward areas have been kept in view

---

[10] Ibid., p. 145.

[11] Ibid., p. 145.

wherever this could be done without giving up essential technical and economic criteria. [12]

Although public policy on industrial location in India has favored small and medium-sized towns, the increase in urban population has been concentrated in large cities.

> The trend in the location of industries in the large-scale sector, however, reveals that the concentration of industries in the metropolitan cities and larger towns has substantially increased over the last decade. This trend is likely to continue unless there is a conscious attempt to enhance the attractiveness of medium and small towns to industrialists by providing in those towns economic facilities and certain basic external economies. This would need to be followed up by a more specific policy regarding location and distribution of industries, which will help direct the future industrialization according to an integrated spatial pattern, aiming at a more balanced development of large, medium and small towns and wider distribution of development foci in the country. [13]

Accordingly the Town and Country Planning Organization suggested the adoption of a number of policy measures to achieve planned dispersal of industries. They recommended that, as a general rule, new industries should not be encouraged in metropolitan cities with a population of more than 500,000 unless their industrial employment falls substantially below 30 per cent of the labor force. Cities in the population range of 200,000 to 500,000 were considered suitable for the location of industries but not for new large-scale industrial enterprises employing over 1,000 workers. The medium-sized urban areas with a population range between 50,000 to 200,000 were favored to receive the large-scale industries. Even when heavy industries were to be located away from existing cities it was suggested that the new industrial centers should be planned as medium-sized urban areas (50,000

---

[12] Ibid., p. 145.

[13] India (Republic), The Town and Country Planning Organization, Ministry of Health, "Note on Location and Planned Distribution of Industries" (New Delhi, Undated), p. 1. (Mimeographed.)

to 200, 000). [14] These recommendations reflect the excessive re-
liance on small-town centered urbanization that is apparent in
recent thinking of Indian planners.

Large cities with some semblance of an adequate infrastructure and a diversified economic base providing a range of
employment opportunity are the only cities enjoying a rapid population expansion coupled with an expansion of per capita income
in some way adequate to support necessary infrastructure inputs.
To make India's numerous smaller cities and towns viable urban
bases for economic expansion will require tremendous investment in infrastructure and in new industrial and commercial activities. The cost of changing the present trend toward expansion in larger cities by making social and economic conditions in
smaller cities and towns competitive thus appears very high.

India's New Towns

One may characterize or define a new town by various criteria. We are concerned here with the planned construction of
urban communities, including new towns designed to promote
planned dispersal from congested urban areas as well as new
urban centers located in the context of urbanization and economic
development processes. In operational terms, our definition has
three major components: a conscious decision with regard to location; an authority--private or public--for preparation of a plan
for the area; and a mechanism either to implement or to exercise a control over the execution of the plan.

A list of new towns planned and under construction that
meet these criteria was prepared from the responses of government and industrial agencies undertaking their planning and development (Appendix B). A substantial majority of the planned new
towns are those built under the sponsorship of industrial corporations in the public sector. New refugee and model towns are
things of the past, and new capital cities are a rare occurrence.
The number of publicly owned industrial projects is likely to increase during the successive states of developmental planning in
India in order to achieve the "socialist pattern of society." If
present trends continue, it is reasonable to expect that the number of industrial new towns will grow rapidly. Figure 1 indicates
the location of new towns listed in Appendix B.

---

[14] Ibid., pp. 1-3.

FIGURE 1

New Towns Selected for Field Work

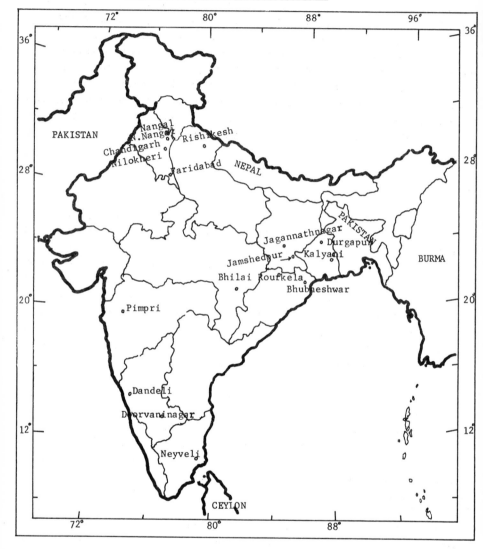

The Annual Report on the Working of Industrial and Commercial Undertakings of the Central Government for the Year 1962-63 lists ten public corporations with a number of projects under construction.[15] Of the thirty projects scheduled to be undertaken by these corporations during the Third Five Year Plan, twenty-five were at different stages of planning and construction on March 31, 1963.[16] Information on the location of these projects and the inclusion of new towns is given in Table 4.

Almost all of the public projects intend to have new towns of their own; of thirty individual plants and projects under construction, twenty-two will have such towns, and for six projects the details had not been fully worked out, the decisions were still pending at the time of publication of the report. For the remaining two projects, Gauhati-Siliguri Product and Haldia-Barauni-Kanpur Pipelines, the need for permanent urban facilities does not arise. Employment in these various public corporation undertakings varies greatly.[17] Not all of the projects which are to have their own towns will construct them at entirely new locations. Some, generally the smaller ones, are building housing and other facilities near existing large cities like Hyderabad and Madras. Even these are not integrated into the existing cities but remain under the control and management of the corporations which build them. The new town idea seemingly has a great appeal and perhaps it has become fashionable to have brand new company towns for governmental enterprises.

Impact of New Towns on Urbanization 1951-61

It is not possible to get accurate estimates for either the existing or the planned population of all the new towns. A rough

[15]India (Republic), Ministry of Finance, Department of Expenditure (Projects Coordination Division), Annual Report on the Working of Industrial and Commercial Undertakings of the Central Government for the Year 1962-63 (New Delhi: March, 1964), p. 7. (Cited hereafter as Annual Report on Public Industrial Undertakings.)

[16]Ibid., loc. cit.

[17]Employment potential has not been worked out for each project. It may be as low as 1,300 (Surgical Instruments Project at Madras) or as high as 18,000 (Heavy Electrical Factory at Bhopal).

TABLE 4

Public Industrial Projects Under Construction and
Proposals for Establishment of New Towns as of March 31, 1963

Name of the Public Corporation	Project(s) under Construction	New Towns Planned?
Heavy Electricals (India) Limited	a) Heavy Electrical Factory at Bhopal	Yes
	b) Heavy Electrical Equipment Plant at Banipur	No known plan and costs for the project not worked out
	c) Heavy Power Equipment Plant at Ramachandrapuram	Yes
	d) High Pressure Boiler Plant at Tiruverumbur	Yes
Heavy Engineering Corporation Limited	a) Heavy Machine Building Project	Yes
	b) Foundry Forge Project	Yes
	c) Heavy Machine Tools Project All at Panchi	Yes
	d) Coal Mining Machinery Project at Durgapur	Yes
Hindustan Organic Chemicals Limited	at Panvel, Bombay	Yes
Hindustan Photo Films Manufacturing Company Limited	at Ootacamund	Yes
Hindustan Teleprinters Limited	at Madras	Not known
Pyrites and Chemicals Development Company Limited	Sulphuric Acid Plant at Sindri	Not known

TABLE 4 (Continued)

Name of the Public Corporation	Project(s) under Construction	New Towns Planned?
Indian Drugs and Pharmaceuticals Limited	a) Anti-biotics Project at Rishikesh	Yes
	b) Synthetic Drugs Project at Hyderabad	Yes
	c) Surgical Instruments Project at Madras	Yes
	d) Phyto-Chemicals Project at Neriamangalam	Not known
Indian Refineries Limited	a) Oil Refinery at Gauhati	Yes
	b) Oil Refinery at Barauni	Yes
	c) Gauhati-Siliguri Product Pipeline	Question not pertinent
	d) Haldia-Barauni-Kanpur Pipeline	Question not pertinent
	e) Calcination of Petroleum at Barauni	Yes
National Mineral Development Corporation Limited	a) Iron Ore Project at Kiriburu	Yes
	b) Iron Ore Project at Bailadila	Not known
	c) Khetri Copper Project	Yes
	d) Panna Diamond Mining Project at Ramkherya and Majhgawan	Not known
Neyveli Lignite Corporation Limited	a) Mining Project	Yes
	b) Thermal Power Project	Yes
	c) Fertilizer Unit	Yes
	d) Briguetting and Carbonization Unit	Yes
	e) Clay Washing Unit	Yes

Source: Table compiled from the Annual Report on Public Industrial Undertakings, pp. 7-24.

"guesstimate" puts the present population in the new towns at about 1.5 million with about half in the refugee towns and colonies primarily developed before 1951 and the rest in the new towns developed thereafter. Relating this figure to the data presented in Table 1, it seems that the role of planned new towns was negligible in the urbanization process of the 1951-61 decade. Of the 1951-61 increase of 16 million in urban population, only 0.75 million persons (less than 5 per cent of the increase in urban population and less than 1 per cent of the total urban population) were living in these towns. All the planned new communities except Chandigarh have been conceived either as small cities or as medium-sized towns. The eventual population planned for most of the towns is 100,000 or below. The projected total population of these new towns could be between 2.5 and 3.0 million, still a minor portion of India's urban population.

A casual glance at particulars of the new towns listed in Appendix B will show that most of them have been planned as special single-purpose towns and that the majority of them are publicly owned single-industry towns. These towns, owned and managed by the industrial units themselves, are all company towns, and with the emphasis on the expansion of publicly owned industries, their number may continue to grow.

The emphasis on single-industry company towns is so great that sometimes various agencies--both public and private--are developing their own independent towns in contiguous areas. Naya Nangal (Fertilizer Corporation's town) adjoins the Nangal town planned and developed by the Irrigation Department of the Punjab Government, and at Durgapur about half a dozen organizations are putting up independent services for their staffs: Hindustan Steel Limited is developing the steel town; Heavy Engineering Corporation, its town; Coke Oven Plant, a colony for their employees; Fertilizer Corporation, its own town; and A.B.V., a private company, has a new town for its workers. Three industrial towns have been developed in and around Bangalore City by Hindustan Aircrafts Limited, Indian Telephone Industries, and Hindustan Machines Tools Limited; the services are also being provided by each sponsoring public corporation individually and not by the Municipal Corporation at Bangalore.

The indiscriminate policy of establishing new industrial towns appears to be unfortunate in the context of rapid urbanization, the imbalance in the occupational structure, lagging investment in infrastructure as well as the availability of undeveloped land in a majority of the existing urban areas. Urbanization is a means for achieving industrial and socio-economic development, and implies an increased level of economic productivity. The unbalanced occupational pattern in India retards the development of the already urbanized areas. To take advantage of the potential that exists in many of the urban areas, it is necessary to promote and create a suitable climate for sustained growth of manufacturing industry. This can be done best by a phased program of investment in infrastructure and the location of industries in these urban areas. New towns can be justified only when comparative cost calculations indicate locational advantages.

The present practice of developing single-purpose, limited-size new towns is questionable even when the location and development of a new urban center may provide a comparative advantage. The single-purpose approach ignores the importance of agglomeration economies, i.e., scale, external, and urbanization economies, and an urban community dependent upon a single industry has a one-sided economic base. As history shows, single-industry towns may prove to be highly unstable during the downward swing of economic cycles.[18]

There is little published literature on the importance of external and scale economies in India. However, there seems to be general agreement that any urban area of less than 100,000 population does not offer opportunities for industrial development. Harris feels that cities with less than one quarter million persons cannot provide a favorable climate for the growth and development of manufacturing industry.[19] External economies are also important for the success of small industries. The study by the International Perspective Planning Team[20] shows that small-

---

[18]See Ira M. Robinson, New Industrial Towns on Canada's Resource Frontier (Chicago, Illinois: Department of Geography, University of Chicago, 1962), Chapter VI, "Economic Base," pp. 91-103.

[19]Britton Harris, "Urban Centralization and Planned Development," in Roy Turner (ed.), op. cit., p. 269.

[20]The International Perspective Planning Team on Small Industries, Report on Development of Small-Scale Industries in India--Prospects, Problems and Policies, to the Ministry of Commerce and Industry, India (New Delhi: Ford Foundation, 1963).

scale factories have developed most rapidly in the large, industrially advanced cities and bigger towns. The Central Small Industries Organization's (Government of India) program to promote and assist small factories "has met its greatest receptivity
and been generally most successful in these locations--not in
small towns, and certainly not in rural areas."[21]

As it is inconceivable that migration to larger urban centers can be completely stopped, and it is even more unlikely that
the migration trend might be reversed, it is too much to expect
that India can do away with the bigger cities. "Those that are
there will be exercising sufficient influence to cause a hierarchy
to be evolved and not the stellar pattern of optimum size cities,
however, much the latter may be desirable."[22] The metropolitan
agglomeration is firmly established in India's urbanization pattern, and, necessarily, is likely to grow in importance.

It is imperative that urbanization policy be evolved on the
basis of a thorough study and analysis of the alternative patterns
of urbanization and their implications. The questions of economies of scale and agglomerative motives cannot be ignored
simply because of such built-in biases and predetermined as-
sumptions in the national Five Year Plans as rural versus urban
and small versus large.

Research Design

This study does not assess all the economies of scale,
comparative costs, etc., which must be considered, but deals
specifically with the cost of building and operating these new
towns. While it must be recognized that political necessity and
social welfare considerations will continue to play important
roles in determining the development design and areal distribution of investible resources, this analysis can provide consider-

---

[21] Ibid., p. 117. See also P. C. Alexander, Industrial Estates in India (Bombay: Asia Publishing House, 1963) pp. 33-34.

[22] India (Republic), Town and Country Planning Organization, Ministry of Health, "Population Growth and Urban and Regional Planning; A Background Paper Contributed to the Asian
Population Conference: 1963," (New Delhi: 1963), p. 13.

able information to the planner when deciding on comparative costs of creating new urban infrastructure and methods of planning to finance it. A careful study of alternative patterns of regional development would, however, illuminate the political process in the hope of improving the quality of political decisions and their implementation.

A list of new towns was prepared, based on the 1951 and 1961 Censuses and the response to the brief pro forma mailed to most of the ministries of the Government of India, planning departments of all the States, and the major public corporations. From this list (Appendix B), seventeen new towns were selected for field work based on two considerations: geographical and functional representation. These seventeen towns are located in nine states, and they include two refugee towns, four steel towns, two state capitals, one fertilizer town, one new town being developed by the Heavy Engineering Corporation, two towns sponsored by the States of Mysore and West Bengal respectively, one town developed in conjunction with a multipurpose irrigation and hydroelectric project, and four other industrial t owns. Data pertaining to the planning procedure and standards set, the costs of development, and the methods of financing were collected for these cities (Appendix A).

To evaluate relative costs in developing new towns, Chapter 2 examines the standards generally adopted for physical planning. Chapter 3 analyzes the costs and financing of these towns. Because housing for government employees constitutes a large segment of the development costs of each city and the methods of financing are representative of the problems of financing other urban development, the economics of this type of housing is examined in Chapter 4. Chapter 5 then offers suggestions for planning and financing India's new urban development. A summary and implications of this study are included in Chapter 6.

CHAPTER II

NATURE OF PLANNING FOR THE NEW TOWNS

Generally, the master plans for the new towns have been prepared by architectural consulting firms, and planning for most of them has been highly concerned with physical aspects of planning, broad land use, pattern, utilities, and other municipal-type facilities. A typical master plan is rarely based upon adequate analysis of the regional economic or social context in which the particular new town will be located. Industrial towns' plans are aimed at providing housing and other facilities for their own employees and the needs of employees from potential ancillary and service industries have been more or less ignored. In fact, none of the new towns provide housing for all the employees of the basic industry within the town. As shown in the following table, percentage of employees provided with housing within the new town may be as low as 12.9 per cent.

TABLE 5

Extent of Housing Provided to Employees in Industrial Towns[a]

Town	Number of Employees	Dwelling Units Built	Per Cent Coverage (3) as % of (2)
Neyveli	26,000	8,377	32.2
Heavy Engineering Corporation's Town at Bhopal	18,200	7,415	40.6
H.A.L. Town at Bangalore	16,500	2,127	12.9
Naya Nangal	2,907	2,254	77.5
Doorvaninagar	8,463	1,508	17.8
Bhilai	24,570	10,997	44.8

[a] 1962 figures

Source: Based on data collected by the author.

Only three of the towns listed in Table 5, the Heavy Engineering Corporation's town at Bhopal, the Hindustan Aircraft Limited town at Bangalore and the Indian Telephone Industries' town at Doorvaninagar, adjoin existing large urban areas; the rest are at entirely new locations. Even in the second category of new towns, the percentage of employees provided with housing within the towns ranges from 32 to 78. Densities in all the new towns are very low and distances between work and home are high even for those workers who live in the towns. For those who commute from the nearby rural areas, the distances become still greater. Since these plants usually run all twenty-four hours, the workers not provided with housing within the planned towns undergo great hardships because of lack of communication, transport facilities, and police protection between the towns and the nearby villages.

This chapter examines three major aspects of planning for new towns: the regional framework, with special consideration of the impact that the location of a new town as well as a major industry may have on its immediate environs; land use provisions; and the planning standards for providing major facilities within the planned communities.

Regional Framework

Planning for most of the new towns more or less neglects the regional setting. No serious consideration of the impact of industrial towns and of large industries on their immediate environs has been attempted. No calculation was made of the employment multiplier to estimate the impact of the development of particular industries upon the immediate region.

Jamshedpur, a steel town developed by the Tata Iron and Steel Company during the middle twentieth century, illustrates somewhat the effect of the employment multiplier. The population of Jamshedpur is about 300,000 with a working population of between 70,000 and 100,000, of which the steel plant employs about 30,000 workers, and other industries associated with iron and steel employ another 12,000 workers. The ratio of the total working force to steel industry employees, therefore, is about three to one. As Jamshedpur is a company town, the growth of that city is controlled by the Steel Company and the multiplier effect may be somewhat lower than usual. Britton Harris estimates that "population multiplier of the <u>initial</u> new employment in a major industry is therefore about 25 to 1."[1] Assuming one worker per average family of five persons, the employment multiplier according to Harris's calculation may be as high as five to one.

This lack of adequate attention to the regional setting in the planning of new towns may reflect the fact that most of these towns were originally planned as single-purpose communities and single-industry towns. Questions of economies of scale, localization, and urbanization were not given any serious consideration. The Committee on Plan Projects observed that:

> In Durgapur, where initially a steel plant was located, a number of ancillary and subsidiary industries have sprung up in an uncoordinated manner, each with its own township, resulting in a conglomeration of several enclaves.

> In Rourkela, a belt of land between the steel plant and the township was left unacquired with the result that this area has developed in a haphazard manner creating slums and unhealthy environment. Such instances also exist in some of the other industrial towns recently built.[2]

While public industrial corporations which developed the new towns did not provide for non-company population at the initial stages of the preparation of master plans, some of them

---

[1] Britton Harris, op. cit., p. 269. The lack of coordination between physical planning and economic setting is evident in most of the industrial towns. For example, the steel town at Bhilai has been planned for an ultimate population of 100,000. According to the projections made by the company early in 1964, the employment was expected to increase from 24,500 in 1964 to about 29,300 by 1966. Assuming the average number of dependents per employee to be four, the population directly dependent upon the steel plant would be about 146,000 in 1966, or about 46 per cent more than the population for which the municipal services would have been planned.

[2] The Committee on Plan Projects, op. cit., p. 3.

re now allotting land for the establishment of subsidiary indus-
ries on an ad hoc basis. Land has been allotted to the respective
tate and central governments for other essential governmental
ervices such as post offices, police stations, and revenue de-
artments. Some residential accommodation is set aside for
other public employees and provisions are made for allocating
and for banks, life insurance corporations, and other needed
ervices. Retail shops are constructed by the company and are
ented for specific purposes to private business or to employees'
cooperatives.

Adequate provision for housing does not exist for those em-
ployed in ancillary industries nor for those who perform necessary services for the residents of the newly planned communities
such as professionals, taxi drivers, rickshaw pullers, petty
vendors, and mechanics. Further, the non-project population
does not enjoy the community facilities of schools, hospitals,
community centers, and clubs, because they are owned by the
company and are intended solely for its employees. A corres-
pondent of The Statesman appropriately sums up the plight of the
non-project population at one of the new towns:

> Non-project people residing at Durgapur who number
> more than half the total population are dismayed be-
> cause, despite past assurances, no provision has
> been made in the new budget to build a hospital where
> they may get medical facilities. In case of an emer-
> gency, a patient has to be removed to either Burdwan
> or Asansol (which is out of many families' reach).
>
> The State transport service was introduced in August
> last but the conveyance problem is as acute as ever.
> The local transport authority has introduced new
> routes without increasing the number of buses. Pro-
> ject employees have been barred from using project
> vehicles for private use since the end of last year and
> consequently the volume of passengers using State
> transport has increased.
>
> The police thana and outposts are inadequately staffed
> and the recent spate of thefts has made the people
> nervous.
>
> With the advent of the summer, water-carriers have
> appeared again on the streets of Benachity and old

Durgapur, the two main market areas.   They charge
19 to 25 nP per bucket of water.[3]

This lack of provisions for non-project employees leads to
unplanned and substandard development on the periphery of new
towns, and if the industrial town is near an existing urban center,
the population of that town increases rapidly over a short period
of time. Facilities which are not provided in the new town crop
up in adjoining areas. When the new town is far from an existing
center, extensive development takes place just outside the town
boundaries. And in both cases, the slums at the outskirts are
growing faster than planned development within the new town.
Areas just outside the new towns usually do not have a filtered
water supply, sewerage, or drainage.

Attempts are now being made to control the problems created by haphazard and unregulated peripheral development. The
State of Punjab enacted the Punjab New Capital (Periphery) Control Act, 1952 (Punjab Act No. 1 of 1953), an Act designed to control and regulate development within a distance of five miles on
all sides from the outer boundary of land acquired for the new
capital at Chandigarh. Section 5 of the Act provides that "Except
as provided hereinafter, no person shall erect or re-erect any
building or make or extend any excavation, or lay out any means
of access to a road, in the controlled area save in accordance
with the plans and restrictions and with the previous permission
of the Deputy Commissioners in writing." And two other states
have enacted similar ordinances.[4] The Committee on Plan Projects, in order to prevent unauthorized construction and slum
pockets at the outskirts of the industrial towns, suggested the en-
actment of interim legislation to protect the periphery of the
areas under development.[5] The usefulness of such Periphery
Control Acts in the absence of adequate arrangements for ancillary industries and supporting population is open to question. At
most it may extend ribbon development a little beyond the current
point.

---

[3] The Statesman (Calcutta), March 16, 1964.

[4] Madhya Pradesh (Periphery) Control Act, 1959 (for the
capital at Bhopal); and the Durgapur (Development and Control of
Building Operations) Act.

[5] The Committee on Plan Projects, op. cit., pp. 7-8.

Most of the new towns were designed by the planners and built by the development authorities as "Garden Cities" incorporating housing at very low densities; most of the houses are single storied with individual gardens that utilize large tracts of land. In view of the high cost of developing urban land in India, these standards appear to be excessive.

How land is devoted to major uses in some of the new towns is shown in Table 6, but it was not possible to get accurate data on land use, either existing or ultimately planned, for many of the towns. Land allocated for residential purposes may be as low as the 9 per cent of developed land at Doorvaninagar or as high as the 45 per cent at Neyveli. Area for roads and streets accounts for about one-third of the total developed land. In Durgapur it is 43 per cent. Land for parks, open space, and recreation ranges from 10 per cent to 69 per cent of the developed land. In many of the new towns (Durgapur, Neyveli, and Bhilai are exceptions) land allocated for parks and open space is more than that provided for streets and roads. Residential use, parks and open space, and roads and streets each account for about 30 per cent of the developed land. The remaining land is for public, semi-public (including education), and other related uses.

Table 6 shows that excessive space has been provided for roads and streets, parks and open space, and this can be seen even more clearly when the data in this table are related to population densities planned for the towns. Table 7 shows acreage per 1,000 persons. This developed area ranges from sixteen to sixty acres, with the minimum and maximum densities varying from seventeen to sixty-one persons per gross acre. The Indian Telephone Industries' town at Doorvaninagar provides the minimum land for residential purposes--3.3 acres per thousand-- while Neyveli has assigned 25.4 acres per thousand for residential plots. Thus, the range of net densities is between 39 persons in Neyveli and 333 persons in Doorvaninagar per residential acre.

The public parks and open space in all the towns total more than 10 per cent of all developed land. Playgrounds are also provided within the educational institutions included under public and semi-public uses in Table 7. Although the suggested standard for public parks and recreation in the United States is ten acres per thousand people, for a country like India four acres per

TABLE 6

Land Use in Some Planned New Towns

Land Use	Dandeli I-Phase Area Acres	%[a]	Dandeli II-Phase Area Acres	%[a]	Durgapur Zones 'A' and 'B' Area Acres	%	Naya Nangal Area Acres	%	H.A.L. Town Bangalore Area Acres	%	I.T.I. Town Doorvaninagar Area Acres	%	Neyveli Area Acres	%[a]	Rourkela Sectors 1 to 8 and 15 to 20 Area Acres	%[a]	Bhadravati New Town Area Acres	%[a]	Bhilai up to December 1963 Area Acres	%[a]	Faridabad Area Acres	%[a]
Approximate planned population in the developed area	25,000		50,000		70,000		10,000		16,000		10,000		50,000		60,000		40,000		60,000		50,000	
Residential	122[b]	30.0	237[b]	37.8	1,017	35.4	104	17.8	80	28.2	33	9.0	1,272	42.6	670	41.5	436	41.4	779	33.8	352	28.8
Roads and Streets	10[b]	2.5	15[b]	2.4	1,219	42.5	119	20.3	66	23.2	77	21.0	935	31.3	334	20.7	232	22.1	544	23.6	345	28.2
Parks, Recreation and Open Space	48	11.8	70	11.2	290	10.1	292	49.9	122	43.0	254	69.2	288	9.7	447	27.7	267	25.4	369	16.0	421	34.4
Education	77	18.9	99	15.8	--	--	10	1.7	--	--	--	--	119	4.0	69	4.3	--	--	94	4.1	28	2.3
Commercial	3	0.7	3	0.5	--	--	1	0.2	--	--	--	--	182	6.1	--	--	11	1.0	54	2.4	30	2.5
Public and Semi-Public	104	25.5	129	20.6	--	--	59	10.1	16	5.6	3	0.8	189	6.3	39	2.4	106	10.1	110	4.8	--	--
Other Uses	43	10.6	73	11.7	345	12.0	--	--	--	--	--	--	--	--	54	3.4	--	--	352	15.3	47	3.8
Total Developed (Excluding Industrial)	407	100.0	626	100.0	2,871	100.0	585	100.0	284	100.0	367	100.0	2,985	100.0	1,613	100.0	1,052	100.0	2,302	100.0	1,223	100.0
Industrial	43		54		n.a.		500		n.a.		n.a.		n.a.		n.a.		531		n.a.		354	
Total Developed (Including Industrial)	450		680		n.a.		1,085		n.a.		n.a.		n.a.		n.a.		1,583		n.a.		1,577	
Undeveloped	--		--		n.a.		1,401		n.a.		n.a.		n.a.		n.a.		n.a.		1,275		888	
Grand Total	450		680		n.a.		2,486		n.a.		n.a.		n.a.		n.a.		n.a.		n.a.		2,465	

[a] Percentage of total developed (excluding industrial) land.

[b] Residential streets only

n.a. = not available

Source: The above table has been compiled from information collected by the author during a field survey of the above towns.

TABLE 7

Acreage Per Thousand Population in New Towns

New Town	Total Area (Acres)	Residential		Roads		Parks and Open Space		Public and Semi-Public		Other Uses		Density-Persons Per Gross Acre
		Acres	% of Total	Acres	% of Total	Acres	% of Total	Acres	% of Total	Acres	% of Total	
Dandeli (1st phase)	16.3	4.9	30.0	0.4	2.5	1.9	11.8	7.3	44.4	1.8	11.3	61
Durgapur	41.0	14.5	35.4	17.4	42.5	4.2	10.1	n.a.	--	4.9	12.0	24
Naya Nangal	58.5	10.4	17.8	11.9	20.3	29.2	49.9	6.9	11.8	0.1	0.2	17
H.A.L. Township at Bangalore	17.8	5.0	28.2	4.1	23.2	7.7	43.0	1.0	5.6	--	--	56
I.T.I. Township at Doorvaninagar	36.7	3.3	9.0	7.7	21.0	25.4	69.2	0.3	0.8	--	--	27
Neyveli	59.7	25.4	42.6	18.7	31.3	5.8	9.7	6.2	10.3	3.6	6.1	17
Rourkela	26.9	11.2	41.5	5.6	20.7	7.4	27.7	1.8	6.7	0.9	3.4	37
Bhadravati New Town	26.3	10.9	41.4	5.8	22.1	6.7	25.4	2.6	10.1	0.3	1.0	38
Bhilai up to 1963	38.4	13.0	33.8	9.1	23.6	6.1	16.0	3.4	8.9	6.8	17.7	26
Faridabad	24.5	7.1	28.8	6.9	28.2	8.4	34.4	0.6	2.3	1.5	6.3	41

Source: The above table is based on information collected by the author from the above towns.

thousand population is the recommended standard.[6] Two towns, Naya Nangal and Doorvaninagar, have standards higher than the accepted standards for the United States. In terms of the international standard for developing countries, all the new towns except Dandeli have higher standards.

It is worthwhile to compare the space standards in the new towns with that which exists in some of the old towns and cities in India. Published material on existing land use in urban areas is scarce. The material available is presented in Table 8. The urban areas have been arranged according to the population size in a descending order. To make Tables 7 and 8 comparable, developed acreage per thousand persons for major land uses has been calculated for some of the old towns. Area for industrial purposes is, however, included under other uses.

Four of the urban areas listed in Table 8--Tinsukia and Dibrugarh in Assam, Agartala in Tripura, and Ootacamund in Madras--are all situated in the mountain regions and, as one would generally expect, they have lower densities and larger space requirements due to physical characteristics. If we exclude these four towns, developed land per thousand persons is less than twenty acres. In the new towns (Table 7), developed land per thousand persons is much higher than twenty acres except in Dandeli and Doorvaninagar. Area per thousand in residential use ranges between 3.4 and 25.4 acres in the planned new towns. The densities in old towns (excluding the four hill towns) are between 50 and 150 persons per acre as compared with 17 and 61 persons in the planned new towns, and the area in roads and streets and parks and open spaces is many times higher in new towns than in the old urban areas. Planning new towns at low densities results in sprawl, and capital as well as maintenance costs increase substantially.

The Committee on Plan Projects, after studying the land uses in the industrial towns, concluded that excessive land was being allocated for roads and streets and open spaces and suggested the following land allocation for a typical sector in a pub-

---

[6] Land Planning Section, Calcutta Metropolitan Planning Organization, "Preliminary Report on Existing Land Uses in the Calcutta Metropolitan District" (May, 1964), p. 14. (Mimeographed.) In this note it is pointed out that an international open-space standard for developing countries such as India is four acres per thousand population.

TABLE 8

Developed Land Per Thousand Persons - Some Old Towns

Urban Area	Total Developed Area (Acres)	Residential		Roads		Parks and Open Space		Public and Semi-Public		Other Uses		Density-Persons Per Gross Acre
		Acres	%	Acres	%	Acres	%	Acres	%	Acres	%	
Calcutta	6.30	3.4	54.3	0.9	15.0	0.5	7.2	0.6	9.1	0.9	14.4	159
Ferozabad	8.23	3.7	45.0	1.1	13.3	0.4	4.3	1.0	12.5	2.0	24.8	122
Rohtak	14.02	7.3	42.2	0.5	3.7	1.3	8.9	1.4	10.2	3.5	25.0	71
Davangere	17.69	7.8	43.9	1.6	9.1	0.4	2.2	2.8	15.7	5.1	29.1	51
Erode	16.17	7.1	43.7	2.7	16.9	0.6	3.8	1.3	7.9	4.5	27.7	62
Sangli	14.70	6.2	41.8	2.1	14.3	1.2	8.3	2.5	17.2	2.7	18.4	68
Dibrugarh	21.49	12.4	57.7	2.6	12.2	0.2	1.1	2.2	10.2	4.1	18.8	47
Bhadravati	19.98	7.7	38.5	0.4	2.1	1.1	5.3	0.8	3.8	10.0	50.3	51
Agartala	24.72	19.6	79.3	1.2	5.0	0.3	1.4	3.2	12.8	0.4	1.5	40
Ootacamund	59.77	31.9	53.4	13.9	23.3	2.1	3.5	6.9	11.6	4.9	8.2	17
Mandya	20.05	8.2	41.0	2.4	11.9	3.4	16.8	2.9	14.3	3.2	16.0	50
Pondicherry	12.84	6.6	51.2	3.7	29.1	0.7	5.2	1.1	8.5	0.8	6.0	78
Tirupathi	11.50	6.9	59.6	1.2	10.6	0.2	1.8	1.3	11.0	1.9	17.0	87
Tinsukia	36.30	15.0	41.3	4.0	11.1	1.3	3.6	2.9	7.9	13.1	36.1	28

Source: Table based on the article by L. R. Vagale, "Basic Issues in Planning of Small Urban Communities and Case Studies of a Few Towns in India," Journal of the Institute of Town Planners, Vols. 33-34 (Jan-Apr. 1963), pp. 12-18. For Calcutta the data in CMPO's study (op. cit.) has been used.

licly owned industrial town:[7]

Residential Plots	45-50 per cent
Roads and Streets	15-20 per cent
Schools including their playgrounds	12-15 per cent
Parks	8-10 per cent
Shopping	2- 4 per cent
Other Uses	Balance
Total	100 per cent

The Committee further suggested net residential densities (sect-
or density) of fourteen to twenty dwelling units serving sixty-five
to ninety-five persons per acre.[8] The gross densities recommended are nine to twelve dwelling units serving forty-five to
fifty-five persons per acre.[9]

The densities and land use pattern suggested by the Committee on Plan Projects have now been adopted as guidelines for
expansion of existing industrial towns in public ownership and for
planning such towns in the future. Since the originally planned
densities were far below the recommended standards, the densities are being increased by construction of multi-storied residential structures alongside existing single-story houses in developed neighborhoods. The trend is to have more or less uniform
densities in all neighborhoods regardless of their size or location, and will cause many difficulties for those entrusted with de-
signing and implementing the modified plans.

A rough parallel exists between the planned new towns and
the older urban areas which are growing in the same time period
without the benefit of a master plan. New unplanned urban areas
all have low densities, are sporadically developed, and leave un-
improved and underdeveloped patches. However, the planned
new towns, also, lack this compact development, because with
increasing urbanization, population pressures increase, land
values go up, and urban land is more intensively used at each

---

[7]The Committee on Plan Projects, op. cit., p. 47. A typical sector as defined by this committee consists of two or three
neighborhoods which can support a secondary school (p. 17).

[8]Ibid., p. 21.

[9]Ibid., p. 21.

successive stage of development. When unplanned urban areas finally feel the need for urban planning, city planning primarily becomes planning for urban renewal and redevelopment. In planned new towns, proper phasing and economically realistic standards could avoid some of these pitfalls.

Standards of Services Provided in the New Towns

In the preparation of master plans for most of the new towns, evaluation of standards for various services within India's social and economic context was not undertaken. Instead, standards were adopted on ad hoc bases during the initial stages of implementation of the plans. The Committee on Plan Projects considered these standards to be unrealistic and recommended service standards for the industrial towns. The ad hoc standards initially adopted by the new towns as well as the ones suggested by the above committee result in very high development costs in terms of Indian economic conditions. Adopted to achieve a better way of urban life, the high costs involved are out of line with Indian fiscal capacity in general and the economic capabilities of the new communities in particular.

Access Standards or Service Radii

In formulating access standards a neighborhood unit has been invariably used. So that a primary school can be supported, the population of a neighborhood is generally three to four thousand persons. Two or three such neighborhoods may be combined to form a sector which can support a high school, or since there are separate high schools for boys and girls, two sectors may be grouped providing high schools for each as well as shopping facilities, a community park, health center, and other such services. The population of such a unit may be between eighteen and twenty thousand. The access standards for neighborhoods and sectors vary widely from one new town to another. The standards recommended by the Committee on Plan Projects are presented in Table 9. These access standards are based on much

31

TABLE 9

Access Standards for Community Facilities

Facility	Walking Distance
Schools	
Nursery	1/4 mile
Primary	1/4 to 3/8 mile
Secondary	1/3 to 1 mile
Recreation	
Tot lot	1/8 mile
Children's park	1/4 to 1/3 mile
Adult's playground	1/2 to 1 mile
Adult's park	1/2 to 1 mile
Groceries and local shopping	1/4 to 1/2 mile
Health Center	1/2 to 1 mile
Post Office	1/2 to 1 mile
Institutional	1 mile
Service Shopping	1 mile

Source: The Committee on Plan Projects, op. cit., pp. 18-19.

higher densities than those now prevailing in the new towns, so that the walking distances are far greater in the new towns studied.

Circulation

Road and street categories are defined by arterial or link roads, principal traffic roads or main distribution roads, local shopping and business streets, neighborhood or sector roads (outer), residential streets or narrow access streets (internal), service lanes, and cycle tracks.

The Committee on Plan Projects has suggested the following standards for different categories of roads and streets:[10]

10 Ibid., p. 30.

Type	Right of Way	Number of Lanes
1. Arterials with Central Median	200' on the periphery of the town, otherwise 160'	One on either side of the median to start with and two on either side ulmately
2. Major Roads (Principal Traffic Routes)	80' to 100'	Two lanes to start with and four lanes ultimately.
3. Neighborhood Roads	45' to 60'	Two lanes.
4. Residential Streets	30' to 45'	Two lanes.
5. Cul-de-sac, not to exceed 600' in length	25' to 30'	Two lanes.
6. Loops	10' to 15'	
7. Service Lanes (for row houses)	15' to 20'	
8. Cycle Tracks	7' to 9'	

These standards for roads and streets provided in many of the new towns and suggested by the Committee on Plan Projects are more or less the same as those suggested for the United States where street planning is based on the ownership of two cars per family. In Sweden, rights-of-way for roads and streets are much narrower than those suggested by the Committee on Plan Projects and the existing road widths in the towns.[11] Planning in Sweden too is based on two cars per family. In Finland, any town plan which provides more than 20 per cent of the area for roads and streets is rejected by the Ministry for Town Planning. When one goes through new towns in India, one finds the streets deserted and very little vehicular traffic; streets seem little used at present.

Phasing of lane construction on arterial roads as suggested by the Committee on Plan Projects seems faulty. When only one lane is built on either side of a median, a breakdown of a vehicle may block traffic. It may be better to start with two lane roads. When more lanes are needed later, both they and a median can be added, making the road a divided highway.

---

[11] General Plan for Stockholm (Town Planning Office of the City of Stockholm, 1952).

Community Facilities

In the company towns, the industry provides community facilities only for their employees. Table 10 lists those provided in some of the new towns.

Standards for community facilities vary so much from one town to another that most seem to be set on ad hoc bases. The population that supports a primary (elementary) school varies from 2,500 at Bhilai to 12,250 at Neyveli. Similarly, the population that supports a high school varies from 4,000 at Naya Nangal to 25,000 at Faridabad. The population per hospital bed ranges from a low of 80 persons at Naya Nangal to a high of 400 persons at Neyveli, and similar variations are found for clubs, shopping facilities, and movie theaters. One reason for these variations in standards may be the fact that some services have to be provided (movie houses, hospitals, etc.) no matter how small the town.

The Committee on Plan Projects, after studying some of industrial towns and considering various factors, suggested the following standards for community facilities:[12]

Education

Category of School	Population Served or Number of Families	Number of Children	Land Requirements
Nursery	500/320	50-60	3 acres
Primary	3,500/640-700	350-400	3 acres
Primary Including Nursery	3,500/640-700	400-500	3 acres
Secondary	9,000/1,900	650-1,000	6-8 acres
Academic College	Not specified	Not specified	15 acres
Technical/Vocational School	Not specified	Not specified	12-15 acres

Community Centers and Clubs - One center to serve two sectors having a total population of about 20,000 persons. Area should be 3-4 acres.

---

[12] The Committee on Plan Projects, op. cit., pp. 31-45.

<u>Recreation</u> - 3 to 4 acres per thousand population.

Tot Lot and Children's Park - 2,000 square feet per
500 persons

Neighborhood Playground - 2 acres
Neighborhood and Sector Parks - 10 acres
Central Park - 30 acres

Medical Facilities

Hospitals

Population	Number of Beds	Size
10,000	30	5 acres (approximately)
25,000	75	10-15 acres
50,000	125	15 acres or above
100,000	2 beds per 1,000 persons	

Health Centers - (Dispensaries to serve out-patients only)

Population	Number	Size
Below 20,000	Nil	Nil
For every 20,000	1	1.0 to 1.5 acres

<u>Shopping</u> - Central shopping in the Town Center and daily shopping in the sector markets at 6 shops per thousand population to be distributed as follows:

Neighborhood - 6-10 shops at 100 to 150 square feet each
Sector - 150 to 200 square feet each
Town or Civic Center large shops

<u>Town Center</u> - To consist of: (1) business and commercial area, (2) entertainment and recreation, (3) cultural area--libraries, museums and art gallery, etc., and (4) civic area having the town hall, town administration, post office, fire station, etc.

Land requirement 0.75 to 1.00 per thousand population.

The standards for community facilities provided in the new towns are generally much higher than those recommended by the Committee on Plan Projects. The Committee, however, did not go into the crucial question of the minimum or optimum size of towns in which the suggested services should be provided.

TABLE 10

Community Facilities in New Towns

Facility	Neyveli	Doorvaninagar	H.A.L. Township at Bangalore	Faridabad	Rourkela	Bhilai	Durgapur	Naya Nangal
Population[a]	50,000	8,000	30,000	50,000	50,000	50,000	50,000	8,000
Education								
Library and Reading Rooms	1&4	1&8	2&3	n.a.	1	1	1	n.a.
Nursery	--	--	--	--	30	--	--	--
Primary/Elementary	4	--	6	10	15	20	8	3
Secondary	4	1[b]	3	2	2	4[c]	3	2[c]
Medical								
Hospitals- Number and Beds	1-116	1-60	1-105	1-150	2-340	2-334	1	1-100
Health Centers Dispensaries	1 with 8 beds	n.a.	6	3	5 with 48 beds	4	2	1
Clubs	2	2	1	n.a.	n.a.	11	1	2
Shopping								
Main	n.a.	--	--	n.a.	--	--	n.a.	--
Sector	18	35	--	n.a.	450	60	n.a.	76
Cinema Movie House	1	1	1	n.a.	1	1	1	1
Community Centers	n.a.	n.a.	n.a.	n.a.	5	2	2	n.a.

n.a. - not available
a - approximate population for which the facilities have been planned
b - combined nursery, elementary and secondary school
c - including one middle school

Source: Based on information collected by the author.

By public utilities we mean such services as water supply, sewerage, sewage treatment, storm water drainage, street lighting, and public transportation systems. It was possible to get data only on standards for water supply. The domestic water supply in new towns varies from twenty to one hundred gallons per capita per day (Table 11).

TABLE 11

Per Capita Water Supply in New Towns

Town	Per Capita Water Supply (Domestic) Gallons Per Day	Remarks
Doorvaninager	15-20	
H.A.L. Township-Bangalore	50	Approximate
Chandigarh	30	
Rourkela	80	
Bhilai	90-100	
Durgapur	60	Approximate

Source: Based on data collected by the author.

The Committee on Plan Projects observed that:

As far as domestic consumption is concerned, we have noted in the industrial township visited by us that the allowances vary from 20 gallons to 100 gallons per capita per day.

Whereas 20 gallons per capita is considered low, 100 gallons per capita is much on the high side. A supply designed to give 40-50 gallons (180-225 litres) per head per day should be satisfactory

This design figure excludes industrial requirements and watering for public parks and open spaces.[13]

---

[13]The Committee on Plan Projects, op. cit., p. 50.

The Central Regional and Urban Planning Organization, in a study of municipal water supply in some urban areas, found that per capita water consumption differs with the size of the urban areas. [14] On the average, it is higher in larger cities and lower in small towns. In 1961, Bombay had the highest per capita water supply at forty-five gallons per day including industrial usage. Among the Class II towns, where population ranges from 50,000 to 99,999, Burhanpur had the highest per capita water supply at fifteen gallons per day.

The water supply systems in most of the new towns, especially the industrial towns, have been designed at high standards, but actual consumption of water is even higher than the design standards because of excessive use for gardening. As water is supplied free in most of the new industrial towns, naturally waste results.

Residential Buildings

Residential buildings account for a substantial portion of capital costs on construction work in a township. Any urban dweller is concerned with the type of house in which he lives. One way to express housing standards is by plot[15] and plinth areas[16] for different types of residential buildings. The data on plot and plinth areas for different types of housing in some of the new towns are presented in Table 12. These towns, except for Chandigarh and Dandeli, are publicly owned industrial towns, but it was not until March, 1960, that the Government of India first set standards for industrial housing. [17] Since land was cheap when acquired, sizes of plot areas were liberally fixed. In all

---

[14] India (Republic) Central Regional and Urban Planning Organization, Ministry of Health, "Some Aspects of Municipal Water Supply on a Few Cities and Towns of India, " Annual Town and Country Planning Seminar, Madras, 1961, Paper No. 16.

[15] Plot area - total site.

[16] Plinth area - area of building coverage.

[17] India (Republic) Ministry of Finance, Department of Expenditure, Memorandum No. 1068/SF/60, dated March 23, 1960.

TABLE 12

Housing for Government Employees in Some New Towns
Plot and Plinth Area in Square Feet*

Income Group Per Month	Rourkela		Durgapur		Chandigarh		Naya Nangal	
	Plot Area	Plinth Area	Plot Area	Plinth Area	Plot Area	Plinth Area	Plot Area	Plinth Area
Rs 50-110	1,200	300-371	1,200	300-400	1,125	449-708	894-1,000	441-466
Rs 111-200	2,400	365-500	2,400	400-600	1,125-1,687	538-908	1,975	885
Rs 201-400	2,400-4,000	460-600	4,800	600	1,687-2,250	538-908	1,975-4,026	1,197-1,226
Rs 401-850	4,000-9,000	880-1,300	8,000	700-1,320	2,250-9,000	908-1,826	3,165-8,097	1,226-1,701
Rs 851-1,600	9,000-16,000	1,400-1,750	12,000	1,320-1,750	9,000-27,000	1,826-2,351	8,097-23,000	1,701-2,667
Rs 1,600-2,500	20,000	2,400-3,830	20,000	1,900-2,400	27,450-29,250	2,661-2,700	24,000-28,000	2,725-3,081
Special-Over Rs 2,500	24,000	4,830	24,000	4,000	41,850-112,500	3,848-11,189	--	--

* Approximate

Source: The table is based on information collected by the author during a field survey.

towns listed in Table 12, space standards for residential plots are very high. The Committee on Plan Projects observed that in industrial towns "... plot areas of individual quarters were rather on the high side probably because land was cheap at the time of initial acquisition. It is seldom realized, that when township grows up, the value automatically appreciates and further acquisition of land for expansion programmes is difficult."[18] They therefore recommended the following plot areas for different housing categories which the industrial towns are following in their expansion programs.

Plot and Plinth Areas for Various Housing Categories[19]

Monthly Salary		Square Feet	
Original Pay Scales	Revised Pay Scales	Plot Area	Plinth Area
Below Rs. 60	Below Rs. 110	900-1,350	350
Rs. 60-150	110-199	1,350-1,800	400
Rs. 151-300	200-399	1,800-2,250	600
Rs. 301-750	400-849	2,925-3,600	900
Rs. 751-1,500	850-1,599	5,850-7,650	1,500
Above Rs. 1,500	Rs. 1,600 and over	5,850-9,000 Plus 900 square feet for servants and garage	2,100 Plus 465 square feet for servants and garage

Summary

On the basis of the foregoing discussion and analysis one can surmise that in the planning of new towns the regional setting has been more or less neglected and that the physical standards and levels of urban facilities in the planned new towns have generally been derived from ad hoc bases without relating them

[18] The Committee on Plan Projects, op. cit., p. 22.

[19] Ibid., p. 23.

to the economic considerations. In fact, planning concepts and the suggested standards in Western countries, especially the United States, have been adopted in a majority of the new towns. Due perhaps to financial and other constraints, even the richest countries of the West have not been able to implement some of the standards adopted in the new towns in India.

In the present chapter no attempt was made to relate the physical facilities to their financial aspects. The next chapter deals with capital, maintenance, and operating costs, and the method of financing these costs in some of the new towns.

CHAPTER III

COSTS AND FINANCING OF NEW TOWNS

Because of the extreme scarcity of resources within the developing countries, the costs of providing infrastructure and other public facilities are of crucial importance in the developmental process. While economic development, industrialization, and urbanization are closely related processes, they may not be wholly interdependent phenomena. Many of India's older urban areas either lack or are inadequately supplied with such basic facilities as water supply, sewerage and drainage, transport and transit, power, and housing. These urban areas are, therefore, not able to support industrialization and urbanization. This lack of industrial activities restricts their tax and revenue base resulting in successive deterioration of municipal services. Rapid growth occurring within these urban areas makes the replacement and modernization of such facilities imperative. Yet in competition with funds for older cities, urban infrastructure created in new towns to support planned industrialization has been developed at high standards which support local industry but which appear to be so expensive and have such a low return on investment that their long-range financing (maintenance costs), as well as future expansion at such high standards, may be impossible.

A very substantial part of the total capital investment in the public sector within the First, Second, and Third Five Year Plans has been for construction of residential buildings and other associated facilities. The Second Five Year Plan (1956-61) expenditure on housing alone was about Rs. 2,500 million,[1] and this figure was expected to be Rs. 4,500 million during the Third Five Year Plan.[2]

---

[1] The Third Five Year Plan, p. 679.

[2] The Committee on Plan Projects, op. cit., p. i (Introduction).

Shortage of available funds is the major constraint on capital improvements, and, once built, capital facilities need proper maintenance. Capital costs influence and largely determine maintenance and operating costs. Therefore initial capital investment in infrastructure and other urban facilities has tremendous impact on future allocation of resources. Capital and operating costs as well as methods of financing should receive careful consideration during planning stages.

This chapter is concerned with the capital, maintenance, and operating costs as well as methods of financing of several new towns for which such data were available. An attempt has also been made to relate these costs to the fiscal capacities of some of these communities. As pointed out in the preceding chapter, the standards adopted in most of the new towns do not vary widely. The per capita costs for most functions differ only slightly for the towns analyzed in this chapter, even though the number of such towns is small, it is felt that they are quite representative.

It was possible to gather detailed costs and financing data for only one new town--Naya Nangal. The analysis based on this information is presented in the Appendix to this chapter.

Governmental and Non-Governmental Costs

Since final decisions in the planning of new towns are made by one or more governmental agencies, and since urban facilities in the new towns are being largely financed by government funds, it should be possible to distinguish between governmental and non-governmental costs. Yet data were available for governmental costs only. Governmental capital costs refer to the costs initially incurred at any level of government--federal, state, local, or their combinations. Since new towns in the past have generally been built by public corporations and financed mainly from public funds, they may also be treated as governmental agencies.

Thus defined, governmental capital costs include land development costs as well as those building construction costs which are financed through public funds. Sometimes public corporations have financed entirely both the land development and the building costs of publicly owned new industrial towns. In some cases, public buildings for federal and state functions -- post offices, state police, federal and state revenue collection units -- have been financed by the state and federal governments. In some new towns, a part of the residential and commercial buildings have been built privately.

Total governmental capital costs and their distribution over land development and building construction for the cities studied are shown in Table 13.[3] Land development averages around 36 per cent of total capital costs, ranging from 19 at Pimpri to 42 at Rourkela. The total capital cost for Pimpri, Rs. 10.8 million, excludes costs for the pumping station and water treatment plant and for personnel, electricity distribution, and street lighting; these costs were debited to the industrial plant account. Thus, land development costs in this case are understated and the percentage of the total would be higher.

Capital Costs in the New Towns

For the purposes of this study, capital costs are divided into two categories: land development costs, and building construction costs.

Land development costs are costs associated with site improvements that must be made before construction of buildings and structures begin. Once site improvements are completed it is, with few exceptions, the responsibility of urban governmental agencies to maintain and operate them. Some public utility func-

---

[3] The capital costs analyzed in this section are estimated costs rather than actual expenditures, as the actual costs were not available. The actuals, even if they were available, would not have served a useful purpose, unless they were related to physical performance over the development periods in respective new towns. I was told by the engineers at most of the new towns I visited that the estimated costs are generally the same as actual expenditures.

TABLE 13

Distribution of Total Governmental Capital Costs Over Land Development and
Building Construction in Selected New Towns[a]

| (Rupees in millions) | Governmental Capital Costs | | | | | |
| | Land Development | | Building Construction | | Total | |
New Town	Rs.	% of Total	Rs.	% of Total	Rs.	% of Total
Chandigarh First Phase	127.2	40.5	186.9	59.5	314.1	100.0
Bhilai First Phase	52.2	31.1	115.6	68.9	167.8	100.0
Rourkela First Phase	60.4	42.1	82.9	57.9	143.3	100.0
Durgapur First Phase	73.9	39.9	111.5	60.1	185.4	100.0
Durgapur Second Phase	35.9	26.9	97.6	73.1	133.5	100.0
Durgapur up to Second Phase	109.8	34.4	209.1	65.6	318.9	100.0
Pimpri	2.1	19.4	8.7	80.6	10.8	100.0
Namrap	6.1	34.9	11.4	65.1	17.5	100.0

[a]The classification of costs into major functions varies in different towns. The cost data have been regrouped to make them comparable. Furthermore, maintenance costs during construction phase, personnel, and audit costs have also been apportioned between land development and building construction. It has been assumed that maintenance during construction may mainly be required for land development functions, especially for water supply, sewerage, drainage, electricity, and roads. These items are interdependent, take much longer to complete, and entail maintenance during their construction. The building and construction items, on the other hand, can be broken into sub-units--a certain number of residential units may be built each year or even in shorter periods--and can be commissioned or brought under use soon after their completion. In this sense these activities require minimal maintenance. The personnel and audit costs have been apportioned according to the ratio between land development and building costs.

Source: Information collected by the author during a field trip in 1963-64. The data for Pimpri and Namrup were obtained from the agencies responsible for these two towns in response to mailed questionnaires.

tions, notably electricity distribution, may be either privately owned or owned by the government. Here, electricity distribution to consumers and street lighting within an urban area is included as one of the functions of an urban governmental unit. So defined, development costs for new towns include the following:

1. land acquisition
2. survey and preparation of contour maps
3. site preparation
4. water supply system
5. sewerage
6. storm water drainage
7. electricity distribution including street lighting
8. roads and bridges
9. landscaping and horticulture
10. temporary works and maintenance during the development stage
11. personnel and audit
12. maintenance of the above during the development phase

Building construction costs refer to costs associated with the construction of buildings after the land has been developed and include residential, institutional, and non-residential buildings.

Land Development Costs

The distribution of capital costs for different land development facilities and services is presented in Table 14. Of these services water supply or roads and bridges invariably occupy the place of prime importance. For public health, water supply, sewerage, and drainage are crucial. When providing economic overheads or infrastructure, electricity and roads must be included. Provision of these functions is necessary to favorable growth of economies in urban areas. As these items constitute more than 60 per cent of total land development costs, the standards should be examined closely for possible changes that could lead to lower costs.

TABLE 14

Distribution of Total Governmental Capital Costs for Land Development Functions

Rupees in Millions

Function/Item	Chandigarh First Phase		Bhilai First Phase		Rourkela First Phase		Durgapur First Phase		Durgapur Second Phase		Durgapur up to Second Phase		Pimpri		Namrup	
	Capital Cost Rs.	% of Total	Capital Cost Rs.	% of Total	Capital Cost Rs.	% of Total	Capital Cost Rs.	% of Total	Capital Cost Rs.	% of Total	Capital Cost Rs.	% of Total	Capital Cost Rs.	% of Total	Capital Cost Rs.	% of Total
Land Acquisition	9.3	7.3	11.5	22.0	8.4	13.9	10.1	13.7	0.2	0.6	10.3	9.4	0.2	9.5	1.3	21.3
Survey of Land	0.6	0.5	0.2	0.4	0.1	0.2	0.1	0.1	Negligible	--	0.2	0.2	--	--	--	--
Site Preparation	--	--	0.5	1.0	--	--	2.5	3.4	1.0	2.8	3.5	3.2	--	--	0.2	3.3
Water Supply	26.3	20.7	8.2a	15.7	10.3	17.1	10.4	14.1	11.0	30.6	21.3	19.4	0.3	14.3	1.3a	21.3
Sewerage	18.1	14.2	5.1a	9.8	8.3	13.7	8.1	11.0	5.7	15.9	13.8	12.6	0.2	9.5	1.3a	21.3
Drainage	13.2	10.4	--	--	0.8	1.3	2.0	2.7	1.8	5.0	3.8	3.4	--	--	--	--
Electricity Distribution and Street Lighting	4.4	3.5	6.0	11.5	7.5	12.4	9.2	12.4	5.9	16.4	15.1	13.7	--	--	1.2	19.7
Roads and Bridges	20.4	16.0	12.2	23.4	7.0	11.6	11.8	16.0	7.1	19.8	18.9	17.2	0.2	9.5	0.6	9.8
Landscaping and Horticulture	5.3	4.2	2.3	4.4	0.7	1.2	1.6	2.2	1.2	3.3	2.8	2.6	--	--	--	--
Temporary Works	--	--	--	--	7.8	12.9	6.4	8.7	--	--	6.4	5.8	--	--	--	--
Personnel and Audit	13.2	10.4	3.0	5.7	3.2	5.3	4.1	5.5	2.0	5.6	6.1	5.6	--	--	--	--
Maintenance During Construction	4.3	3.3	2.1	4.0	3.7	6.1	4.1	5.5	--	--	4.1	3.7	--	--	--	--
Other Development Costs	12.1	9.5	1.1	2.1	2.6	4.3	3.5	4.7	--	--	3.5	3.2	1.2	57.2	0.2	3.3
Total Land Development Costs	127.2	100.0	52.2	100.0	60.4	100.0	73.9	100.0	35.9	100.0	109.8	100.0	2.1	100.0	6.1	100.0

a Includes drainage.

Source: Author's field survey.

Building Construction Costs

The relative importance of individual items included in building construction costs is shown in Table 15. Residential buildings usually account for more than three-fourths of the total building construction costs. Chandigarh is the exception with only 41 per cent. As the new Punjab State capital, it required the construction of non-residential buildings such as the Assembly House, High Court, and Secretariat. The total government costs are necessarily much higher in Chandigarh and result in a comparatively lower percentage for housing costs. Privately built housing at Chandigarh is substantial, about half of the total, and is non-existent in any other new town listed in Table 15.

Per Capita Governmental Capital Costs

Per capita governmental costs provide a better basis for cost comparisons. Per capita costs for seven cases (six new towns) are shown in Table 16,[4] while the detailed costs for these towns are given in Appendix C.

Per capita total governmental costs range from Rs. 2,352 in Pimpri to Rs. 4,384 in Chandigarh. The new town at Pimpri,

---

[4] Per capita costs have been calculated as follows: Three different denominators or population bases have been used to obtain a fair estimate of per capita costs, for realistic comparison. Total costs for each function have been related to the population for whom the facilities have been planned or built: (1) The land acquisition costs have been divided by the population ultimately planned in each new town. (2) Since housing has been or is being constructed for a fixed number of families, the cost of residential buildings has been divided by the approximate population that may be living in such houses. This has been calculated by multiplying the number of houses built by 5 although the average size of the urban family in India is a little less than 5. (3) The remaining land development, as well as other functions, has been assumed to cater to the needs of the populations planned in each of the new towns. These populations correspond to the cost data used in Table 20. The capital costs on these functions have been divided by the population planned for particular stages.

TABLE 15

Distribution of Total Governmental Capital Costs for Construction of Buildings

Rupees in Millions

Function/Item	Chandigarh First Phase		Bhilai First Phase		Rourkela First Phase		Durgapur First Phase		Durgapur Second Phase		Durgapur up to Second Phase		Pimpri		Namrup	
	Capital Cost Rs.	% of Total	Capital Cost Rs.	% of Total	Capital Cost Rs.	% of Total	Capital Cost Rs.	% of Total	Capital Cost Rs.	% of Total	Capital Cost Rs.	% of Total	Capital Cost Rs.	% of Total	Capital Cost Rs.	% of Total
Residential Buildings	76.3	41	90.6	78	64.8	78	83.9	75	81.6	83	165.5	79	7.6	87	9.8	86
Non-Residential Buildings	86.8	47	18.3	16	12.0	15	21.0	19	10.4	11	31.4	15	0.7	8	1.6	14
Personnel and Audit	19.5	10	6.7	6	4.3	5	6.2	6	5.6	6	11.8	6	--	--	--	--
Other Costs	4.3	2	--	--	1.8	2	0.4	Negligible	--	--	0.4	Negligible	0.4	5	--	--
Total Building Construction Costs	186.9	100	115.6	100	82.9	100	111.5	100	97.6	100	209.1	100	8.7	100	11.4	100

Source: Author's field survey.

49

TABLE 16

Per Capita Governmental Capital Costs in Some New Towns

Function/Item	Per Capita Capital Costs in Rupees						
	Chandigarh First Phase	Bhilai First Phase	Rourkela First Phase	Durgapur First Phase	Durgapur up to Second Phase	Pimpri	Namrup
Land Acquisition	19	115	84	145	104	35	133
Survey of Land	4	4	2	2	2	--	--
Site Preparation	--	8	--	4	35	--	22
Water Supply	175	136	172	148	213	--	125
Sewerage	120	85[a]	139	116	138	59	134[a]
Drainage	88	--	13	29	38	33[a]	--
Electricity Distribution and Street Lighting	29	100	124	131	151	--	115
Roads and Bridges	136	204	116	168	189	47	57
Landscaping and Horticulture	35	37	12	24	28	--	--
Temporary Works	--	--	130	92	65	--	--
Personnel and Audit	88	50	53	59	62	--	--
Maintenance During Construction	29	36	62	59	41	--	--
Other Development Costs	81	19	43	50	35	235	19
Total Land Development Costs	804	794	950	1,027	1,101	409	605
Residential Buildings	1,572	2,416	1,728	2,229	1,830	1,704	1,960
Non-Residential Buildings	1,789	488	320	559	347	159	322
Establishment and Audit	130	112	72	88	117	--	--
Other Non-Development Costs	89	--	49	9	4	80	--
Total Building Construction Costs	3,580	3,016	2,169	2,885	2,298	1,943	2,282
Total--All Functions	4,384	3,810	3,119	3,912	3,399	2,352	2,887

[a] Includes Drainage.

Source: Per capita costs have been estimated from the data collected by the author.

established by Hindustan Antibiotics Limited in conjunction with a penicillin factory, is located near Poona City and it now forms a part of the Poona Town Group which is somewhat analogous to a greater metropolitan area in the United States. Started in 1953-54, most of the facilities were completed by 1955-56. The rest of the towns are still in initial processes of development. Electricity distribution and street lighting costs at Pimpri were borne by the State Electricity Board of Maharashtra and by Hindustan Antibiotics Limited, and the cost of water for Pimpri in Table 16 does not include the pumping house and the water treatment plant as these were debited to the company's plant account. Finally, since the new town at Pimpri is very small, with a planned population of only 6,000, the area in roads is only 6.5 per cent of the total planned area, against about 30 per cent in the other new towns. A lower price level when Pimpri was built also contributed to the very low per capita total cost. Chandigarh, the State Capital for Punjab, is dominated by the Capitol development consisting of a group of major buildings including the High Court, the State Assembly, the Secretariat, and the State Governor's office and residence. The high expenditure on non-residential buildings is due to the huge capital costs of these buildings. If this expenditure is subtracted from the total per capita costs for Chandigarh, and if Pimpri is excluded, the range in per capita total costs of the sample new town is no longer substantial.

Per capita land development and building construction costs should be treated separately. Development functions are generally the responsibility of the urban government, and are financed in the long-run by property and non-property taxes, public utility and intergovernmental revenues. Municipal governments are not usually required to provide all the remaining items, particularly housing, and so these items are not proper municipal functions. Subsidized public housing may be provided by local governments, but this depends upon public policies at higher echelons of government which provide a substantial portion of funds for this purpose.

Per capita land development costs average Rs. 913, but these costs vary widely from one new town to another. Pimpri, with the lowest cost of Rs. 409, is followed by Namrup with Rs. 605, but these figures exclude some development functions. Part of the cost of water supply and all electricity costs are not included in Pimpri, while per capita costs at Namrup exclude personnel and maintenance--costs which have been debited to the plant account. Furthermore, Pimpri and Namrup have been planned for only 6,000 and 10,000 persons respectively. As the area in roads is proportionately much smaller, and presumably street construction is also of lower quality, the per capita cost on roads is substantially lower in these two towns.

For building construction items, per capita capital costs for housing range from Rs. 1,572 to Rs. 2,416. The weighted average per capita cost for all houses in the new towns analyzed in Table 16 is Rs. 1,871 when personnel and audit costs are excluded, or Rs. 1,943 when the proportionate share for personnel costs is added. Per capita costs for essential municipal services and housing are approximately Rs. 2,850. Thus the average cost of urbanization per family, when an average size of 5 persons is assumed, is about Rs. 15,000.

Per Acre Governmental Capital Costs

Per acre costs relate to financial decision-making for new towns. As development costs largely determine land values, they should form the basis for land disposal policies in urban areas in general and in new towns in particular. Land prices, as well as annual charges, must be determined in relation to land development costs. If the cost of residential and most non-residential buildings--excluding educational, religious, and charitable institutions--is added to development costs, the total costs approximate the real estate tax base in a new town. The per acre cost can thus be useful in formulating land disposal as well as revenue policies.

Per acre costs for some of the new towns are shown in Table 17[5] where per acre total governmental capital costs range

_____

[5] Per acre costs for different items have been derived as follows: Total land acquisition cost has been divided by the total land acquired. For the remaining items, total land developed has been used as the denominator. The respective cost data correspond to the amount of land developed. The cost for each item has, therefore, been divided by the amount of land developed. For residential buildings at Chandigarh, a slightly different method has been used. About 50 per cent of the housing at Chandigarh is privately built. The total developed area for the first phase is 5,000 acres. The cost data available to us is for government housing only. These costs have been divided by 2,500 on the assumption that half of the acreage is for private housing.

TABLE 17

Per Acre Governmental Capital Costs in Some New Towns

Function/Item	Per Acre Capital Costs in Rupees						
	Chandigarh First Phase	Bhilai First Phase	Rourkela First Phase	Durgapur First Phase	Durgapur up to Second Phase	Pimpri	Namrup
Land Acquisition	1,084	581	840	970	985	2,100	3,185
Survey of Land	131	102	69	53	48	--	--
Site Preparation	--	195	--	936	953	--	525
Water Supply	5,258	3,555	6,409	3,835	5,755	2,950	2,998
Sewerage	3,613	2,227[a]	5,174	3,012	3,723	1,650[a]	3,218[a]
Drainage	2,638	--	466	741	1,036	--	--
Electricity Distribution and Street Lighting	872	2,602	4,623	3,399	4,072	--	2,758
Roads and Bridges	4,075	5,314	4,328	4,356	5,099	2,360	1,374
Landscaping and Horticulture	1,054	971	440	611	762	--	--
Temporary Works	--	--	4,826	2,389	1,744	--	--
Personnel and Audit	2,650	1,312	1,963	1,514	1,662	--	--
Maintenance During Construction	855	930	2,294	1,588	1,112	--	--
Other Land Development Costs	2,420	491	1,612	1,295	945	11,740	446
Total Land Development Costs	24,650	18,280	33,044	24,634	27,896	20,800	14,504
Residential Buildings	30,521	39,362	40,173	31,065	44,726	76,090	23,501
Non-Residential Buildings	17,367	7,943	7,438	7,772	8,490	7,110	3,856
Personnel and Audit	3,898	2,907	2,693	2,285	3,168	--	--
Other Non-Development Costs	860	--	1,136	130	95	3,590	--
Total Building Construction Costs	52,646	50,212	51,440	41,252	56,479	86,790	27,357
Total--All Functions	77,296	68,492	84,484	65,886	84,375	107,590	41,861

a. Includes Drainage.

Source: Per acre costs have been estimated from data collected by the author.

53

from Rs. 41,861 to Rs. 107,590. The average per acre cost for all the new towns listed in Table 17 is Rs. 76,437, while average land development and building construction costs per acre are Rs. 25,362 and Rs. 51,075 respectively.

It can be expected that densities and per acre costs move in the same direction, and that per capita costs vary inversely by density. This should be particularly true for land development costs and per capita and per acre costs should be inversely related. These relationships, however, may be modified by: relative quality and quantities of different services in the new towns; and price variations from one region to another.

The number of towns for which comparable costs have been analyzed in Tables 16 and 17 is small. These new towns have been planned at low densities. Except Pimpri, where the overall density is fifty persons per gross acre, the densities in the remaining towns range from twenty-four to thirty-seven. Pimpri still has the lowest per capita and highest per acre costs. Rourkela has the second highest density, while its per capita costs are the third lowest and per acre costs the second highest. For the rest, the relationship does not necessarily hold.

Maintenance and Operating Costs

Capital facilities require proper maintenance and entail recurring costs. Capital costs largely determine maintenance and operating costs and are crucial in financial as well as physical planning. These costs may be defined to include the following: interest on initial capital, depreciation, or debt service (interest on initial capital and repayment of principal); and, costs associated with maintenance and operation of capital facilities.

It is preferable to use interest and depreciation charges rather than debt service as the former is a far superior index of annual costs; debt service is an accurate estimate of cash expenditures only during the life of the debt. Debt service is useful in planning long term as well as short-term cash budgets and is dependant upon prevailing interest rates and the period for which the loan may or can be raised. Duration of any particular loan may or may not synchronize with the life of the facility financed through such a loan. Loans under the various housing schemes sponsored by the federal and state governments and the Life Insurance Corporation of India are generally to be repaid in twenty to twenty-five annual installments, but the life of the residential buildings financed through such loans may be thirty, forty, or fifty years.

Use of interest and depreciation charges, provides a better estimate of annual costs for the interest charge determines the cost of using capital funds, and depreciation represents the cost of using a particular asset. Interest charges and depreciation are used to represent part of the annual maintenance and operating costs throughout the rest of this study.

Depreciation should take into account the salvage value of an asset, but for simplicity and convenience, salvage value has been ignored. There are different methods for depreciation accounting that depend upon the purpose served. Historical rather than replacement costs may be used and the annual depreciation charge may be based on a straight line method of depreciation accounting.

Major repairs, renovations, and replacement of certain components of a large facility may require high but non-recurring expenditures at some future date and the annual cost must account for such expenditures. This can be done by adding the present value of the estimated future expenditure to the initial capital cost, or by applying the average annual maintenance costs at a rate that takes these extraordinary expenditures into account.

A third component of maintenance and operating costs consists of salaries for the personnel responsible for maintenance and operation, materials and contingencies, repairs, and taxes and insurance.

While these costs are not taken into consideration in the decision-making process for building planned new towns in India, usually the maintenance expenditure during the period of construction of some of the facilities is both estimated and included in the capital cost estimates. When construction is completed, an authorization of a certain fixed percentage, usually 2.5, of total capital costs generally is requested as a lump sum maintenance budget. This does not provide for some of the personnel costs, particularly the staff responsible for administration and management of various facilities such as accounting, and billing and collection of charges for water, electricity, rents; nor does it provide for interest and depreciation.

In most new towns accounts for maintenance expenditures are not kept and relevant data are fragmented and incomplete. Only Naya Nangal maintains proper accounts for current expenditures and allocates interest, depreciation, and personnel costs for the major functions.

An attempt has been made to discover some rules of thumb for determining the annual maintenance and operating costs for the new towns under study. These may be best expressed as ratios between maintenance and operating, and capital costs.

First, let us look at the ratios of Naya Nangal shown in Table 18.[6] Annual maintenance and operating costs for all functions are about 11 per cent of the total capital costs for Naya Nangal. Of this total 5.2 per cent is for interest, 2.9 per cent for depreciation, and the remaining 2.7 per cent for salaries, contingencies, and repairs. The average annual costs, expressed as percentage of capital costs, are higher for the land development than for the other functions.

The Fertilizer Corporation generally calculates interest charges at 5.5 per cent per annum. It built 736 residential units under the Subsidized Industrial Housing Scheme of the State of Punjab. Fifty per cent of this cost was a twenty-five year loan at 4.5 per cent interest and the remaining half was a grant so that interest charges for residential buildings at 4.8 per cent are lower than the usual rate.

Depreciation is based on the straight line method. The residential buildings are of two types with average expected lives of thirty and twenty years respectively. The annual depreciation charge works out at 3.4 per cent. The life of the electric supply system is assumed to be 16 years and depreciation is calculated at 6.3 per cent. Water supply and sewerage (including drainage) are depreciated at 5 per cent and 4 per cent respectively. The respective charges for the schools and the hospitals (including equipment) are 5.3 per cent and 5.7 per cent.

---

[6] These ratios have been calculated from the data collected from the Fertilizer Corporation of India's project at Naya Nangal. They are based on the annual accounts for the year 1961-63.

TABLE 18

Maintenance and Operating Costs as Per Cent of Capital Costs for Naya Nangal During the Financial Year Ending March 31, 1963

| Function/Item | Maintenance and Operating Costs as Per Cent of Capital Costs | | | | | |
| | Interest | Depreciation | Salaries | Contingencies | Repairs | Total (2+3+4+5+6) |
1	2	3	4	5	6	7
Land[a]	5.5	--	1.3	0.3	0.2	7.3
Water Supply	5.5	5.0	2.3	3.0	0.5	16.3
Sewerage and Drainage	5.5	4.0	1.2	--	0.2	10.9
Electricity Distribution and Street Lighting	5.5	6.3	7.5	9.3	1.7	30.3
Roads and Bridges	5.5	--[d]	1.2	--	0.6	7.3
Land Development	5.5	2.2	2.0	1.5	0.4	11.6
Residential Buildings	4.8	3.4	1.2	0.2	0.2	9.8
Non-Residential Buildings--						
Education[b]	5.5	5.3	1.2	0.2	1.3	13.5
Hospitals and Public Health[c]	5.3	5.7	1.2	0.2	0.6	13.0
Others	5.0	3.3	1.3	0.3	--	9.9
Building Construction	5.0	3.6	1.2	0.2	0.3	10.3
All Functions	5.2	2.9	1.6	0.8	0.3	10.8

a Includes landscaping and horticulture.
b Salaries of the educational staff and direct contingencies excluded.
c Salaries of the hospital staff and direct contingencies excluded.
d Depreciation on roads is not included in the annual costs.

Source: Information collected during a field survey.

Water supply, electricity, and non-residential buildings, especially educational and medical institutions, entail much higher maintenance and operating costs. Their functions are not easily susceptible to generalization, and may vary from one town to another. Maintenance and operating costs as a percentage of capital costs usually do not vary widely for housing and the other land development functions.

Land Development Functions (Excluding Public Utilities)

The annual maintenance and operating costs may be assumed to be between 8 and 10 per cent of the capital costs. The annual costs consist of interest at 5 to 5.5 per cent, [7] depreciation at 1 and 2 per cent; [8] and salaries, contingencies, and repairs at 2 to 2.5 per cent. [9] The annual costs for these functions may have to be financed mainly from either real estate taxes or from revenues related to land policy.

Public Utilities

The annual costs (consisting of interest at 5 to 5.5 per cent; depreciation at 4.5 to 6.5 per cent; and salaries, contingencies, and repairs at 5.5 to 8 per cent) may be assumed to be between 15 and 20 per cent of capital costs.

---

[7] The interest rate on long-term government borrowings in 1965 was 4.8 per cent. (Reserve Bank of India, Bulletin, February 1965.) The Life Insurance Corporation on its advances for 20-25 years for such purposes charges interest at 5.5 per cent.

[8] Since land does not depreciate, a lower depreciation rate has been assumed for all development functions taken together. Depreciation on roads has been assumed to be about 2 per cent per year.

[9] These costs for Naya Nangal are a little less than 2 per cent. Since the facilities are almost new, two items under this heading (contingencies and repairs) are lower in the initial years. The percentage has therefore been assumed to be between 2 and 2.5 per cent per year.

Buildings

The annual costs for maintenance and operation of residential and non-residential buildings may be assumed to be between 8.5 and 10.5 per cent. They consist of interest[10] at 4.5 to 5.5 per cent; depreciation at 2 to 2.5 per cent;[11] and salaries, contingencies, and repairs at 2 to 3 per cent.[12]

Per Capita Annual Costs

Annual per capita maintenance and operating costs have been estimated for seven cases and are presented in Table 19.

TABLE 19

Estimated Annual Maintenance and Operating Costs
in Some New Towns

| New Town | Per Capita Annual Costs | |
	Low Estimate[a] Rs.	High Estimate[b] Rs.
Chandigarh First Phase	351 (190)[c]	438 (238)
Bhilai First Phase	305 (257)	381 (321)
Rourkela First Phase	250 (214)	312 (268)
Durgapur First Phase	313 (260)	391 (326)
Durgapur Up to Second Phase	272 (234)	340 (293)
Pimpri	188 (169)	235 (211)
Namrup	231 (205)	289 (257)

[a]Calculated at 8 per cent of capital cost.

[b]Calculated at 10 per cent of capital cost.

[c]Figures in parentheses exclude costs of buildings except housing.

---

[10]See footnote 7. Lower rates of interest have been assumed because of subsidized housing for industrial workers and other low income housing. State and central governments advance funds generally at between 4 and 5 per cent.

[11]The life of residential buildings has been assumed to be between forty and fifty years.

[12]See footnote 9.

Two types of estimates have been made: a low at 8 per cent of capital cost, and a high at 10 per cent of capital cost. The low estimates range from 188 to 351 while the high estimates vary from 235 to 438. When building construction costs, except for housing, are excluded, then the ranges are from 169 to 260 and from 211 to 326 respectively.

Methods of Financing Capital Costs

Initial capital for new towns is largely included in funds provided by the Government of India for approved projects included in the Five Year Plans. The extent and kind of participation by the federal government, however, differs for the two state capitals and the new towns built by the public industrial corporations. For the new towns at Kalyani and Deandeli in the States of West Bengal and Mysore the initial capital has primarily been provided by the respective state governments.

The State Capitals

The extent and kind of financial participation by the federal government for Chandigarh and Bhubneshwar was neither decided nor agreed to at the time of formulation of the master plans or while preparing the capital improvement programs. Information is not readily available as to what proportion of the total capital has been, and will be, provided by the federal government, and on what conditions. The Planning Commission communicates to the two state governments the probable amounts that the latter may expect to receive in the course of the forthcoming Five Year Plan periods. The state governments then, to the extent feasible, include the balance of requirements in their own budgets each year.

The assistance given by the federal government to the state governments of Punjab and Orissa for building the capitols is either in the form of outright capital grants or long-term loans. The contributions of the state governments are in the form of grants. Once the land in certain parts of the planned new town is developed, the private sale of plots provides additional funds for further improvement.   Thus, the total expenditure of Rs. 125.2 million at Chandigarh to the end of the First Five Year Plan (March 31, 1956) was financed as follows:[13]

		Millions	
Contribution by the State Government	Rs.	30.0
Grant from the Planning Commission	Rs.	30.0
Loans from the Rehabilitation Ministry, Government of India, for the rehabilitation of refugees from West Pakistan.[14]	Rs.	30.0
Loan from the Government of India for housing	Rs.	4.4
Sale of Plots	Rs.	30.8
Total	Rs.	125.2

The grants and the loan assistance provided by the federal government is rarely earmarked for specific purposes and their duration, and interest thereon, was not known to any of the administrators interviewed by the author.   Investigation of the state budgets did not reveal any record of interest or loan payments to the federal government, and the entire financial data and accounts are scattered and impossible to collate.   Analysis suffers from these limitations.

The New Industrial Towns

The initial capital required for building new towns in conjunction with public industrial projects and the capital for plants themselves is provided collectively by the federal ministries

---

[13] The Government of Punjab, "New Revised Project Estimate of the New Capitol of Punjab Chandigarh" (Chandigarh: Undated), p. 33. (Typed Manuscript.)

[14] Punjab was one of the states partitioned on the eve of India's independence into West Punjab (now in Pakistan) and East Punjab (now in India).   The majority of the refugees from West Pakistan settled in East Punjab.   The Punjab State was thus the recipient of large numbers of grants and loans from the federal government during the early years after independence.

sponsoring or administratively in charge of the different corporations. The funds thus provided may represent the federal government's subscription to the share capital or may be long-term loans. The interest payments are generally deferred during the first five years while the rate of interest is around 5 per cent per annum. In one or two cases, the public corporations have taken advantage of industrial housing schemes, and then a part of the initial capital was given as an outright grant by the federal and/ or state government with the balance financed by government loans.

Sources of Current Revenues

None of the planned new towns under study have so far been incorporated as municipalities. Their revenue systems thus differ substantially from the revenue structure in the municipalities and the municipal corporations in India. Taxes on real estate have not been levied in any of the new towns. Non-property taxes and license fees are non-existent. The main sources of revenue are:

> rent or lease charges on land, rent of residential and non-residential buildings, water charges, conservancy charges (for sewerage), electricity charges, receipts from horticultural operations, such as sale of trees and grass, fees from educational institutions, and receipts from medical and public health services excluding conservancy charges.

Rent of Land

In Chandigarh and Bhubneshwar, most land for private purposes has been sold outright with no provision for subsequent annual charges either for land or improvements thereon. The Punjab State Government has announced that "they would not levy house tax or property tax or apply the Rent Restriction Act to the town (Chandigarh) for a period of 25 years. "[15] The management of the public industrial projects do not sell the land but may lease it for varying periods depending upon the purpose or use, and in addition to an initial down payment, annual ground rent is charged from the leasee.

Rent of Residential Buildings

There are three different methods for determining the rent for a particular residential or a non-residential unit depending upon who occupies it. The charge is lowest if occupied by a public employee. When a building is rented to a governmental organization other than the one developing the new town--such as federal government offices and residential accommodation for their staff--the rent charged is higher than·the one charged the employees, but lower than the rent charged for the same property for non-governmental parties.

The rent charged from the employees is determined in accordance with Fundamental Rule No. 45-A, which provides that when a government employee is provided with residential accommodation owned or leased by the government, the former shall pay "rent for the residence such rent being the standard rent as defined in clause III above or 10 per cent of his monthly emoluments, whichever is less. "[16] The standard rent is calculated on the capital cost of the residence in one of two ways.

> (i) A percentage of such capital cost equal to such rate of interest as may from time to time be fixed by the Secretary of State in Council plus an addition for

---

[15] V. P. Malhotra, "A Note on Chandigarh Capital Giving Its History and Administrative Set Up" (Chandigarh: Undated), p. 17. (Mimeographed.)

[16] The Accountant General, Posts and Telegraphs, Compilation of the Fundamental Rules made by the Secretary of State in Council under Section 96-B of the Government of India Act, including Orders, etc., issued by the Secretary of State, Government of India, Auditor General, etc., and the Supplementary Rules made by the Governor General in Council including Orders, etc., Third ed. (Reprint), Vol. 10 (Simla: 1959), pp. 79-80.

municipal and other taxes in the nature of house or property tax payable by Government in respect of the residence and for both ordinary and special maintenance and repairs such addition being determined under rules which a Local Government may make;

(ii) 6 per cent per annum of such capital cost, whichever is less. [17]

The standard rent thus calculated is for a full year and is divided by twelve to arrive at the monthly rent. The capital cost, however, excludes the cost of land.

The annual rent from other governmental organizations is either the standard rent--6 per cent of the capital cost, but the capital cost in such cases includes the cost of land, its preparation, and improvements thereon--or 8 per cent of the cost of land, site preparation, and buildings. [18]

Charges for Water

Most of the new towns do not have a metered water supply Only in Chandigarh is the entire water supply metered and charges based directly on consumption. In a few public industrial towns meters have been installed on a very small fraction of the water connections. Employees are provided water free of charge or at substantially lower rates than those charged the non-project population. Rates for water supply in some of the new towns are shown in Table 20.

The charges for water, when based on the number of taps in a building (sometimes the diameter of the tap is also considered), attempt indirectly to measure the average consumption of water. It is, however, interesting to note that in the industrial towns developed by the public corporations, the cheaper water supplied to the employees is a deliberate policy of management

---

[17] Ibid., p. 79.

[18] The new towns developed by Hindustan Steel Limited charge the non-departmental governmental organizations at 8 per cent of the capital cost inclusive of land costs.

TABLE 20

Charges for Water in Some of the New Towns in India

Name of the New Town	Whether Water Supply Metered or Not	Charges for Water	
		Employees	Non-Project Population
Chandigarh	Metered	Rs. 1.00 per 1,000 gallons	Rs. 1.00 per 1,000 gallons
The Fertilizer Corporation's Town at:			
Naya Nangal	Not Metered	Rs. 1.25 per month for house type I rising to Rs. 8.00 for house type VII.	Rs. 3.50 per month for house type I to Rs. 8.00 for house type IV.
Namrup	Not Metered	Free	Not available
Steel Towns at:			
Rourkela	Partially Metered	Free	Other Governmental Organizations - the monthly rates for residential buildings are Rs. 1.00 for the first and Rs. 0.50 for each subsequent tap; Rs. 1.00 for each garden tap or Rs. 2.00 per 1,000 gallons in case of metered supply. Non-Governmental Parties - the monthly rates are Rs. 3.00 per water tap or Rs. 2.00 per 1,000 gallons if meters are fitted.
Bhilai	Not Metered	Free	Not available
Durgapur	Not Metered	Free	Not available

Source: Information collected from the towns.

Per capita consumption, as well as waste of water, is bound to be very high and the domestic water supply systems in most of them are planned on the basis of eighty to a hundred gallons per capita per day, while at Chandigarh it is thirty gallons per day. All the industrial towns have been planned as garden cities and attempt to provide individual gardens to each household. The indiscriminate use of water for gardening, as the watertaps may be kept running most of the 24 hours, is the main cause of abnormally high consumption of water in these towns.

Conservancy Charges

The conservancy charge for sewerage and drainage services is based on the number of toilets, but like the water supply, conservancy charges are either non-existent in the industrial towns, or when levied, are at much lower rates to employees than to others. At Rourkela, the charges are Rs. 1.0 per toilet from the employees and Rs. 2.0 from the non-governmental parties. At Chandigarh, conservancy rates are uniform.

Electricity Charges

Public enterprises generally purchase power at bulk rates from the State Electricity Boards and set up their own distribution systems within the planned new towns. Charges to employees are again lower than charges to others. Naya Nangal charges Rs. 0.19 per unit for the first 40 units and Rs. 0.12 per unit in excess of 40 units from its own employees but Rs. 0.22 per unit from the others. Similarly at Rourkela, the charges for the employees are about Rs. 0.08 per unit whereas the non-project population pay Rs. 0.14 per unit. The lower rate for a monthly consumption of over 40 units at Naya Nangal is presumably designed to favor the higher income group of employees because they use more electricity than the lower salaried employees. At Chandigarh, the State Electricity Board supplies and distributes the electricity directly to the consumers at uniform rates.

Horticultural, Educational, and Medical Receipts

These three items need no explanation, but it may be pointed out that the employees of the industrial corporations receive free medical attention and hospital facilities. Revenues are mainly charges received from other governmental employees and facilities are generally not available to non-governmental persons. At Chandigarh, primary and high school facilities are not the responsibility of the Estate Office carrying out the municipal functions but are under the Education Department of the State Government while medical and hospital facilities are the responsibility of the State Health Department. The Estate Office is concerned with public health--sanitation, food inspection, conservancy, etc.

Financial Implications of New Towns

In the preceding sections we analyzed capital costs for seven towns and the weighted average capital costs in these new towns were found to be Rs. 2,856 per capita and excluded non-residential buildings such as schools, hospitals, health centers, and other civic buildings. The total capital costs per capita may be divided into three major categories and are shown in Table 21.

TABLE 21

Average Per Capita Capital Costs and Maintenance
and Operating Costs in New Towns

Major Function	Capital Costs (Rs.) Per Capita		Annual Maintenance and Operating Costs (Rs.) Low		High
Land development (excluding public utilities)	627	@	8%- 50	@	10%- 63
Public utilities	286	@	15%- 43	@	20%- 57
Housing	1,943	@	8.5%-165	@	10%-194
Total	2,856	@	258		314

Whether costs are high and imply that standards are also high can best be considered by relating the annual maintenance and operating costs for these functions (Table 21) with the level of incomes in the new towns. Per capita income in the urban areas during the year 1960 was Rs. 437.[19] The average per capita income for the new towns at Durgapur, Bhilai, and Naya Nangal during 1963-64 has been estimated by the author to be about Rs. 450.[20] If the estimates of annual maintenance and operating costs and personal incomes are valid, the former constitutes between 57 and 70 per cent of the latter.

Municipal finance theory, as well as sound financial principles, demand that land development costs should be financed mainly through municipal taxes, the public utility costs through charges for these services, and the housing costs through rental receipts for residential buildings. The financing of annual maintenance and operating costs from local resources would require that municipal taxes should roughly equal 11-14 per cent, utility charges 9-13 per cent, and housing another 37-43 per cent. Prima facie these costs cannot be born by the inhabitants of these new towns and must be financed through substantial subsidy.

An important variable arising in our analysis is the future ability of the community to pay for the municipal services and other facilities in the new towns. Since capital facilities in the new towns will last for a number of years to come, it is realistic to relate the maintenance and operating costs to future ability to pay. Let us assume that the expected average life of all the facilities is thirty years and let us further assume that the per capita incomes in the new towns will be rising at a constant rate during the next thirty years. The average per capita incomes during the next thirty years would then be roughly equal to the

---

[19]National Council of Applied Economic Research, Urban Income and Savings (New Delhi: 1962), p. 110.

[20]For these three towns, information on number of employees in the different corporations and their pay-scales was ascertained. Assuming that the employees did not have any other source of income except salaries and wages, income per employee was estimated. Income (average) per employee in the three public corporations was found to be between Rs. 2,200 and Rs. 2,250. These incomes were then divided by 5, the average size of the family, assuming one wage earner per family, to arrive at per capita personal incomes.

level of incomes at the midpoint, or during the fifteenth year. It is, therefore, reasonable to relate the average maintenance and operating costs with average level of incomes during the life of the assets or the facilities in the new towns.

Per capita income in India increased from Rs. 267 in 1950-51, to Rs. 326 in 1960-61.[21] During this period the per capita income increased by 22 per cent or at the simple rate of growth of 2.2 per cent per year, and at 2 per cent annual cumulate rate of growth. The per capita income during the years 1961-76, according to targets stated in the Third Five Year Plan, is to increase from Rs. 330 which later estimates put at Rs. 326, to Rs. 530[22] or a 60 per cent increase in the 1960 level of per capita income. This gives a simple rate of growth of 4 per cent, or a compount rate of growth of 3 per cent per year. Applying this rate of growth to the level of urban incomes in 1960, the per capita income in urban areas might be Rs. 700.

Annual maintenance and operating costs have been estimated in Table 2 to be between Rs. 258 and Rs. 314 per person in the new towns. In all likelihood the costs fifteen years hence would be closer to Rs. 314 than to Rs. 258. Given these estimages of per capita income and the annual maintenance and operating costs, the annual costs of the new towns would still be 45 per cent of income. The municipal taxes, public utilities, and housing costs would constitute 9, 8, and 28 per cent respectively of the average urban income, and demonstrate that the planned new towns studied will not, in all probability, become self-supporting in the foreseeable future.

So far our analysis has not taken into account intergovernmental fiscal relations, the actual operating expenses for educational, medical and public health facilities, or the tax and non-tax municipal revenues which industry and commerce within the community might contribute. It is felt that the picture would remain more or less unaltered if these variables were introduced. First, the costs of electricity distribution, water supply, sewerage and drainage and other development costs for the areas occupied by the industrial plants are not included in the capital

---

[21]Department of Economic Affairs, Ministry of Finance, Government of India, Indian Economic Statistics (New Delhi: August, 1963), Part 1, p. 12.

[22]The Third Five Year Plan, p. 28.

costs on which the per capita costs have been based. Intergovernmental fiscal relations do not play a significant role in the finances of local bodies in India. During the year 1956-57, the per capita grants to local bodies in Delhi were about Rs. 2.[23] Grants for education and for medical and public health facilities may constitute about two-thirds of the total amount of grants to local bodies from higher echelons of government. Per capita annual expenditure for education and medical facilities (excluding interest payments and depreciation) during the year 1962-63 at Naya Nangal was Rs. 14 and Rs. 70 respectively. Naya Nangal is considered representative of other new towns, and since these items are not included in the calculation of maintenance and operating costs, the introduction of this variable--intergovernmental fiscal relations--would have further added to the annual costs shown in Table 21. Since the commercial section has little significance within the planned new towns, its contribution to municipal revenues would have been negligible.

Relationship Between Current Costs and Current Revenues: A Case Study of Naya Nangal

To demonstrate many of the problems associated with operating India's new towns a case study of Naya Nangal was undertaken. The maintenance and operating costs of Naya Nangal during the financial year 1962-63 were typical of other new towns and are presented in Table 22.

The maintenance and operating costs for providing urban facilities to the residents of the new town at Naya Nangal were Rs. 4, 957, 296 during the financial year 1962-63. The comparable costs during the preceding year were not appreciably different. The ultimate population for which the new town has been

---

[23] J. P. Sah and Ved Prakash, "Grants-in-aid, " (Financing the Plan Series, Preliminary Paper No. 2), (New Delhi: Fiscal Planning Section, Town Planning Organization, Ministry of Health, Government of India, January 1959), p. 34. (Mimeographed.)

TABLE 22

Maintenance and Operating Costs for the Period April 1, 1962 to March 31, 1963 for the New Town at
Naya Nangal Built by the Fertilizer Corporation of India, Limited

Amount in Rupees

Function/Item	Salaries	Contingencies	Repairs, etc.	Depreciation	Interest	Total	Per Cent of Grand Total
General Administration							
Estate Office	62,880	--	--	--	--	62,880	1.3
Civil Works Maintenance							
Staff	130,822	--	--	--	--	130,822	2.6
Accounts Staff	14,331	--	--	--	--	14,331	0.3
Security Staff	102,974	--	--	--	--	102,974	2.1
Other Staff	7,488	8,828	--	--	--	16,316	0.3
Sub Total	318,495	8,828	--	--	--	327,373	6.6
Land	--	21,963	--	--	421,010	442,973	8.9
Water Supply	76,533	97,209	17,601	137,836	182,130	511,309	10.3
Sewerage and Drainage	--a	--	6,004	149,220	188,763	343,987	7.0
Electricity Distribution and Street Lighting	111,859	140,385	24,676	86,036	60,049	423,005	8.5
Roads and Bridges	--a	--	15,685	--	134,399	150,084	3.0
Landscaping and Horticulture	94,992	594	11,294	2,594	1,690	111,164	2.3
Education	109,771	26,131	4,795	21,490	26,091	188,278	3.8
Medical and Public Health	426,621	268,729	9,857	84,945	78,682	868,834	17.5
Residential and Non-Residential Buildings (excluding education, hospital, and public utility buildings)	--a	26,061	47,776	627,298	889,204	1,590,339	32.1
Grand Total	1,138,271	589,900	137,688	1,109,419	1,982,018	4,957,296	100.0

a   Included Under General Administration.

Source: The table has been compiled from the information collected by the author from the Office of the Deputy General
Manager and the Finance and Accounts Department of the Fertilizer Corporation of India Limited at Naya
Nangal.

planned is 10,000 persons. The population in 1961 was 7,987.[24] The Fertilizer Corporation has already constructed 2,252 residential units. One may, therefore, assume that the total current costs of Rs. 4,957,296 would more or less be the same even if the population during 1962-63 was 10,000. This gives us a per capita maintenance and operating cost of Rs. 496 for that year. To put it another way, the annual cost per family was about Rs. 2,480, but do not include transportation costs. The transport service within the new town is run by the Corporation itself and is available to its employees at subsidized rates.[25]

The current revenues during the year 1962-63 (Table 23) amounted to Rs. 792,697 and were 16 per cent of the current costs. Per capita and per family revenues during the same year were Rs. 79 and Rs. 395 respectively.

TABLE 23

Revenue Receipts During the Financial Year April 1, 1962,
to March 31, 1963, for the New Town at Naya Nangal
Built by the Fertilizer Corporation of India, Limited

Major Head	Revenue Receipts Rs.
Rent from land, residential, and non-residential buildings	476,712
Water charges	58,131
Conservancy charges	36,512
Electricity charges	110,604
Horticulture - sale of trees, vegetables, etc.	40,894
Education - fees from schools	52,846
Medical and Public Health excluding Conservancy	16,998
Total Revenue	792,697

Source: Information collected by the Author from the Office of the Deputy General Manager and the Finance and Accounts Department of the Fertilizer Corporation of India, Limited, at Naya Nangal.

[24] Census of India, Paper No. 1 of 1962, Final Population Totals, p. 226.

[25] The employees with a monthly income of Rs. 250 or more can use the bus for coming to and going from place of work by paying Rs. 10 per month. They are entitled to use the Corporation's automobiles by paying Rs. 25 per month for the above trips. For private local trips, the offical cars can be used against payment of Rs. 0.50 per mile.

As noted earlier, annual costs per capita and per family were Rs. 496 and Rs. 2,480. The per capita deficit, therefore, was Rs. 417. The per capita deficits on some important functions during the year 1962-63 were as follows:

Function	Per Capita Deficit (Rs.)
Water Supply	45
Electricity	31
Conservancy	31
Education	14
Medical and public health	87
Rent from land and buildings	156

The deficits for conservancy and rent from land and buildings are exclusive of personnel and other costs listed under general administration in Table 22.

Deficits occur in each major function. Total revenues are only slightly higher than total contingencies. If the rent for land, residential, and non-residential buildings is excluded from the total revenue, the balance is not even adequate to pay for the maintenance and operating costs of the water supply system designed for domestic use in the new town at Naya Nangal.

The new towns are very expensive propositions. They cannot be expected to be self-financing in the initial years, but it is doubtful if deficits of the order indicated above will ever be eliminated at Naya Nangal if present policies remain unchanged. It is even unlikely that sizeable reductions can be effected in the magnitude of the deficit. Even if policies regarding the levying of different charges can be completely overhauled, urban facilities during the foreseeable future will have to be subsidized substantially.

In every urban area the industry within the community generally comprises the largest group of taxpayers, and to that extent the industry subsidizes the municipal facilities. It is questionable, however, whether the industry can afford and should pay for the community facilities to the extent indicated by our examination.

It has been thus demonstrated that the annual maintenance and operating costs in the planned new towns are very high relative to the financial capacity of the residents. This, in turn, implies that the standard of services provided in these new towns is also very high. The main reason for high planning standards is that the planning of new towns is based on predetermined standards rather than on any rational investment criteria--e. g., economic analysis, rate of return analysis, benefit-cost analysis.[26]

The emphasis on physical and land use aspects in the planning of these new towns is not different from the current planning practice elsewhere. The Town and Country Planning Organization, M nistry of Works, Housing and Urban Development, Government of India (an advisory body for the State Departments of Town Planning having the responsibility for allocating federal assistance funds to the state governments, for hiring professional staff, and for the preparation of master plans) is "primarily concerned with the physical aspects of local urban development and puts heavy emphasis on land use plans as a terminal product of a short term crash program. "[27]

Urban planning in India relies heavily on the concepts and techniques of planning evolved in the nineteenth and the twentieth centuries in North America and Western Europe, notably the United States and Britain. The attempt is to transplant rather than transform Western standards to suit Indian conditions. Brown and Gilbert point out that in the United States "standards as they have developed historically, have primarily reflected the interest of the professional administrator but have in fact tended to be accepted as rules by the planners who make use of them."[28] Functional standards emerge as a result of the "codified aspirations of an interest group in response to situations in which re-

---

[26] For discussion of criteria for public investment, see W. H. Brown, Jr., and C. E. Gilbert, Planning Municipal Investment (Philadelphia, Pennsylvania: University of Pennsylvania Press, 1961), pp. 253-85.

[27] Leo Jakobson, op. cit., p. 46.

[28] W. H. Brown, Jr., and C. E. Gilbert, op. cit., p. 272.

sources are to be distributed."[29]   Once such standards are near realization, they tend to be raised.   Professional standards are not adequate criteria for investment planning for urban development.

The Committee on Plan Projects undertook the study of industrial towns at the request of the Ministry of Steel and Heavy Industries and the Planning Commission because the sponsors felt that construction costs of the industrial towns in the public sector were excessive.[30]   The Committee noted that:

> As excessive capital outlay on townships has an adverse effect on the cost of production, the Ministry of Steel and Heavy Industries and the Planning Commission felt that a detailed study of the existing townships be made with a view to evolving norms and standards for the planning of future townships and expansion of the existing ones.[31]

The Report of the Committee, however, does not make reference to what the costs have been in the new industrial towns in the public sector; what should be the criteria for investment planning in municipal services; or what should be the method of financing the initial improvements and the maintenance and operating costs in the long run.   There is a chapter in the Report on "Avenues of Cost Reduction,"[32] but this deals in general terms with such items as "scope of cost reduction," "cost reduction in the planning of townships," "diversification of specifications," "greater stress on pre-fabrication," "payment to contractors," and so on.   The Committee has recommended planning and other standards for the guidance of public corporations concerned with

---

[29]H. J. Gans, "Recreation Planning for Leisure Behavior" (unpublished Ph.D. dissertation), quoted in Brown and Gilbert, op. cit., p. 273.

[30]The letter forwarding the Report from the Minister for Food and Agriculture, Government of India, to the Minister for Home Affairs and Chairman, Committee on Plan Projects, dated May 6, 1963.

[31]The Committee on Plan Projects, op. cit., p. 2.

[32]Ibid., pp. 68-84.

building municipal and housing facilities for their employees. Its main concern was to suggest norms and standards that should be adopted for the industrial towns. The suggested standards are little different from those recommended in planning textbooks in the United States and England.

A realistic appraisal of land use, densities, and other standards is needed from still another standpoint. If the new towns are to be considered as nodes or growing points for further industrial and urban development, the standards in the new towns have to be related to urban development in general. With various subsidized housing schemes, the physical standards, the cost ceilings, and the extent of subsidy vary from one scheme to another. Slum clearance and redevelopment schemes have different maximum ceilings and methods of determining the element of subsidy. The suggested standards for lowest-income housing for government employees are, however, much higher than the permissible standards for any other low-income or industrial housing schemes.

Some professional planners and planning educators in India are critical of current planning practice. S. Saeedush Shafi expresses his concern in the following words:

> In general, the establishment of new towns on a mass scale would be an expensive proposition for a country like India. But, on the other hand, where large industries, particularly in the public sector are to be established, it should be possible to develop new towns. However, in the planning of these our standards are likely to be basically different from those in the Western countries. For one thing, our towns should be more compact and, instead of individual open spaces, we should emphasize community open spaces; consequently their overall densities would be higher than those of similar towns in Europe. Indeed, most of the new towns built recently in India are not designed as compact urban units; most of them have too low a density and are scattered, thereby increasing the initial investment and the recurring cost of maintenance.[33]

---

[33] S. Saeedush Shafi, op. cit., p. 6.

The magnitude of the urbanization problem is such that within the limited resources available the minimum acceptable standards must be curtailed considerably, and an attempt has to be made to use whatever facilities are provided as extensively as possible. If urban facilities are to be used extensively, it is imperative that their maintenance and operations receive very careful consideration and that the different functional programs that constitute urban development -- provision of basic public health facilities, infrastructure, housing and other facilities -- have to be assigned very different priorities with perhaps the first two receiving the highest priorities. Nevertheless, much of the population of India may have to be content with community water taps, community latrines, and community bathing facilities. Slum improvement programs in urban areas may have to be substituted for slum clearance and redevelopment programs. Educational and other facilities may have to be used in two, three, or more shifts. This acceptance of realistic standards may prove to be difficult "because it defies everything that planners hitherto have considered as an absolute minimum for socially acceptable human settlement."[34]

The lack of coordination between physical and financial planning is also apparent as inadequate attention is given to revenue programing or arrangements for long-term financing of capital improvement programs, and is reflected in the benevolent attitudes on the part of the agencies entrusted with development of the new towns, particularly the industrial towns.

There have been few opportunities for private capital to finance commercial and residential development except at Chandigarh and Bhubneshwar. It is strongly felt that if the construction of commercial buildings and housing for middle- and upper-income groups had been left mainly to the private sector, the demand on public resources would have been eased and private savings and investment mobilized.

Arrangements for taxation do not exist, nor are there any plans in the near future for levying taxes or adopting other revenue measures to finance the development functions. Even where charges are levied for public utilities--water supply and electricity--they are not based on the consideration that these services have to be self-supporting.

---

[34]Leo Jakobson, op. cit., p. 51.

Summary

The costs associated with building new towns are considered to be excessive in relation to the financial ability of these communities. Based on the capital costs, per capita annual maintenance and operating costs have been estimated to be between Rs. 258 and Rs. 314. The per capita annual income in some of the new towns has been estimated to be around Rs. 450. The annual costs thus approximate between 57 and 70 per cent of the residents' personal income in the new towns. Under the present financing arrangements, none of the normal municipal facilities are self-supporting, and deficits occur in each and every public service. The excessive costs substantiate the findings in the preceding chapter, i.e., the standards for urban planning are too high.

HOUSING FOR GOVERNMENT EMPLOYEES IN NEW TOWNS

Investment in housing accounts for about half of the total governmental expenditure for developing new towns and entails the largest amount of recurring deficits. Therefore, the means for developing housing must be emphasized when formulating overall urbanization policy as well as when considering specific housing problems such as desirable standards, or whether the housing should be rented or sold.

The organizations responsible for the planning and development of new towns have constructed most of the houses within the planned areas. About fifty per cent of the total residential units in the two state capitals have been built by the respective state governments for their employees; all the housing in the new towns has so far been built by the public corporations responsible for their development.

Practically, initial housing developments must be the responsibility of development agencies for housing is either scarce or non-existent where the new towns are to be located. Economic expediency makes it desirable to provide public housing in order to attract personnel to the new urban areas; private individuals or organizations may not be willing to undertake this task during the early stages of development. It is sometimes essential to provide subsidized public housing to families with low incomes in both new and old urban areas.

Houses built in the new towns by the state governments and the public corporations usually have been rented to their employees and very rarely to non-employees. They are not for sale, and inquiry shows that the public agencies are not in favor of selling these houses either to employees or non-employees. This policy, to rent rather than to sell, gives greater control over the company employees; undesirable employees not only may be dismissed from the employ of the company but also may be evicted from company housing and therefore forced to move out of the new town.

Housing Standards

Public policy on housing standards explicitly recognizes that housing for certain categories of government employees must be subsidized. The types of houses recommended for public employee categories based on salary groups are decided by the state public works departments in the two state capitals. Their standards are in terms of plot size, built-up area, the number of rooms, and internal facilities, and are not prescribed in terms of maximum ceilings on capital costs or the unit rates for different types of residential structures.

Housing standards in industrial towns were initially decided by the different public corporations on ad hoc bases. Early in 1960, the Committee of Economic Secretaries in different ministries of the Government of India considered the question of housing for government employees in the public sector industries, hoping to reduce costs and effect savings in investment. They also recognized that "the projects would also have to incur recurring cost to the extent that the rents charged are lower than the reasonable return from the capital invested in housing."[1] Deficits were to be in the form of concealed subsidies. The Committee recommended the following six categories of housing.[2]

---

[1] India (Republic), Department of Expenditure, Ministry of Finance, Office Memorandum No. 1068/SF/60, dated March 23, 1960, p. 1.

[2] Ibid., p. 1.

Type	Salary Group (Monthly)	Plinth (Built-Up) Area in Square Feet
I	Below Rs. 60	365
II	Rs. 60-150	400
III	Rs. 151-300	600
IV	Rs. 301-750	900
V	Rs. 751-1,500	1,500
VI	Above Rs. 1,500	2,100 plus 240 square feet for servants and 225 square feet for the garage.

In addition to these physical standards in terms of plinth or built-up area, the Committee recommended that the average monthly subsidy for any one hundred assorted houses should not exceed Rs. 1,500. This concealed subsidy was to be calculated in the following manner:

Having regard to the cost of construction on the basis of the 6% of return on the cost of construction, land and development and on the assumption that rent fixed would be subject to a ceiling of not more than 10% of the emoluments, the concealed subsidy in the form of difference between 6% return and the rent at 10% of pay should work out approximately to Rs. 1,500 per month for 100 assorted houses, in the proportion of say, 80% for types I-III, 13.5% for type IV, 6% for type V and 0.5% for type VI. It may be necessary to vary the percentage of various types to suit the requirements of individual projects, but specifications, scales of accommodation, etc., should be so adjusted that:

(a) the amount of such subsidy for the said 100 houses of mixed types should, as far as possible, not exceed Rs. 1,500 per month, and

(b) the accommodation of persons drawing over Rs. 300 per month should not normally be subsidized.[3]

---

[3] Ibid., p. 2.

Another office memorandum supplementing the one dated March 23, 1960 was issued by the Finance Ministry in August 1960. It stated that:

(i) In calculating the economic rent it has been stipulated that the cost of land and development should also be added to the cost of houses. For this purpose an addition of 10% to the cost of respective houses may be allowed and every effort made to keep the cost within this limit. If, however, this is not possible in any case the detailed reasons for the same should be brought to the notice of the sanctioning authority.

(ii) For houses to be constructed in areas where the cost of construction is higher than in Delhi the standard subsidy of Rs. 1,500 for 100 assorted houses might be increased by 15% for every increase of 5% in the construction cost index (compared to Delhi), limited to a maximum of 75%. [4]

Thus, if the cost of construction in a particular new town is 25 per cent more than the construction cost in Delhi, the concealed monthly subsidy could be the maximum permissible or Rs. 2,626 (175 per cent of Rs. 1,500) for one hundred assorted houses for the government employees.

Pay scales of federal government employees were revised upward effective July 1, 1960, and the public corporations followed this lead. Consequently, the Ministry of Finance issued another office memorandum in August, 1963 modifying the salary groups entitled to the six categories of houses. [5] The report of the Committee on Plan Projects on industrial townships was published in May, 1963, and the Committee adopted the earlier standards outlined by the Finance Ministry in their memoranda dated March 23, and August 29, 1960. In addition, they recommended

---

[4] India (Republic) Department of Expenditure, Ministry of Finance, Office Memorandum No. EL(11)-PC/60, dated August 4, 1960.

[5] India (Republic) Ministry of Finance (Works Branch), Office Memorandum No. 14(16)/60-W, dated August 29, 1963.

plot areas corresponding to the six housing types.[6] The standards are now being followed more or less uniformly by the different public corporations.

The rental or the subsidized housing policy for employees of the public corporations is based on two considerations: the method of calculating the subsidy; and the quantum of maximum permissible subsidy. In calculating the subsidy the 6 per cent annual return on capital invested in housing is assumed to be the "economic rent" and is defined as a periodic charge for financing public housing on a no profit-no loss basis; the 10 per cent of salary of the government employees is considered as a desirable charge or the "social rent." The difference constitutes the subsidy. One may ask, however, does 6 per cent of the capital cost of land, development, and construction of houses represent the true economic rent; and is it reasonable to assume that the social rent or the desirable charge should not be more than 10 per cent of the government employee's salary? A corollary to the second question may be: is it justifiable to keep this 10 per cent constant for all public employees and not to consider the salary groups to which they may belong?

The total capital costs which form the basis of calculating the subsidy must be considered. Capital invested in housing represents both the cost of land and development, and the houses. The Finance Ministry's Memorandum No. EL(11)-PC/60, dated August 4, 1960, suggested that 10 per cent of the cost of houses may be taken as the representative cost of land and development. Residential development in the new towns planned prior to the issuance of the above memorandum and built by public corporations excluded the cost of land and development for preparation. This was sanctioned by Fundamental Rule No. 45, which provides that the "standard rent" should be calculated at 6 per cent of the capital cost, excluding the cost of land.[7]

The relationship between the cost of land and development and the construction of houses depends upon: the land use plan (land allocated for various uses); standards at which such facilities as roads, parks, open spaces, public utilities, and other community facilities are provided; and the housing standards and their density. The costs associated with land and development

---

[6] The Committee on Plan Projects, op. cit., p. 23.

[7] The Fundamental Rules, op. cit., p. 77.

on the one hand and residential buildings on the other determine the above relationship and may vary from one new town to another. The suggested 10 per cent of housing cost as the cost of land and development presupposes very intensive and high density residential development. Cost of land and development in relation to construction costs of residential buildings is much higher than the 10 per cent assumed by the Finance Ministry. When the ratio of land and development cost to housing cost is higher than 1:10, the actual subsidy may be more than that permissible.

Furthermore, the ratio of land and development cost to construction cost varies by housing types. The relationship for different categories of housing is dependent upon: the ratio of built-up land to the plot areas (plot coverage); and the quality (expressed in terms of cost per square foot of the built-up area) of different housing types. Generally the plot coverage is higher in the lower categories of houses and vice versa. The quality of the houses represented by the average per square foot cost of the built-up area is slightly higher for higher categories of housing. Thus, the residential units in the three steel towns may be grouped into four broad categories depending on the per square foot average rates for their construction.

TABLE 24

Per Square Foot Cost of Construction of Different Housing Types in the Three Steel Towns

Housing Type	Average Per Square Foot Rate for the Built-Up Area (Rs.)		
	Rourkela	Durgapur	Bhilai
I	13.54	16.19	16.85
II	13.95	17.60	16.26
III	14.53	20.27	16.89
IV	16.08 and 20.04	n.a.	n.a.

Source: The Superintending Engineer, Hindustan Steel Limited, "Information Supplied to the Committee on Plan Projects" (Ranchi: Undated), p. 55. (Mimeographed).

Both the plot coverage and the quality of the different housing types result in different ratios of land and development costs to construction costs, although generally this ratio is lower for

84

housing provided to those with lower incomes and substantially higher for the better paid government employees.

Finally, personnel costs and maintenance charges during the construction phase represent sizeable expenditure and may constitute 6-12 per cent of total capital investment in new towns. It is, therefore, reasonable to allocate and add the cost of these two items to the land development and construction costs when calculating investment in public housing in the new towns. The total costs thus arrived at should form the basis for deriving the economic rent. Present practices lead to under-estimation of economic rent as well as subsidies for all types of residential units.

Whether a 6 per cent return on capital invested in housing represents a reasonable annual economic rent will now be considered. A 6 per cent rate probably has been adopted from its use in Fundamental Rule No. 45 under which the annual standard rent is calculated. However, the calculation of the standard rent takes into account the prevailing interest rate, municipal and other taxes, as well as ordinary and special maintenance and repairs, but excludes the cost of land and development included by the Finance Ministry in their memoranda of March 23 and August 29. The relevant sub-section F.R.45-A.III(b) reads:

> In the case of residences owned by Government, the standard rent shall be calculated on the capital costs of the residence and shall be either--
>
> (i) a percentage of such capital cost equal to such rate of interest as may from time to time be fixed by the Secretary of State in Council plus an addition for municipal and other taxes in the nature of house or property tax payable by government in respect of the residence and for both ordinary and special maintenance and repairs, such addition being determined under rules which a Local Government may make, or
>
> (ii) 6 per cent per annum of such capital cost, whichever is less. [8]

The Fundamental Rules first became effective on January 1, 1922. Perhaps before 1922 these rules were in force under different

---

[8] The Fundamental Rules, p. 79.

names. Many of them may have been promulgated during the nineteenth and early twentieth centuries. Fundamental Rule No. 45 in its present revised form was made applicable from August 3, 1927.

The interest rates were lower in 1922 and land and construction costs during the next forty years rose at rates higher than the increase in general price level. In all likelihood, the housing standards were lower then. It is reasonable to assume that the 6 per cent ceiling in Fundamental Role No. 45A adequately covered the maintenance and operating costs including interest payments. Put another way, the standard and the economic rents may not have been substantially different when this rule was adopted.

Perhaps Fundamental Rule 45A provided that rent charged should either be 10 per cent of salary or the standard rent, whichever is less, because only a few categories of houses for government employees were to be subsidized and when the 10 per cent of salary was higher than the standard rent, the government employee was not to be put to a disadvantage. If this is the case, the adoption of the 6 per cent return on capital invested in public housing for employees of the public industrial corporations by the Finance Ministry in the 1960's seems to be highly unrealistic and grossly unrepresentative of the true economic rent.

Economic Rent, Rent Charged, and Subsidy for Different Housing Types

The economic rent, as defined here, is equal to the annual user costs of the maintenance and operating cost. The annual economic rent thus consists of: the annual interest on capital (costs); the annual depreciation; and the annual costs associated with the management and maintenance of publicly built housing. On the basis of the detailed data for Naya Nangal, and other relevant information, it is estimated that the annual maintenance and operating costs for residential buildings is between 8.5 and 10 per cent of capital costs.

Calculations of the economic rent, the rent charged, and the element of subsidy for different categories of housing for the government employees in four new towns--Chandigarh, Rourkela, Durgapur, and Naya Nangal, have been made and these detailed calculations of economic rent are shown in Appendix D, Tables 1-4. Cost of land and development for Chandigarh, Rourkela, Durgapur, and Naya Nangal has been estimated at Rs. 0.80, 0.90, 0.80, and 0.70 per square foot respectively, and have been derived from Table 13. The net per acre development costs of water supply and electricity, including the proportionate share for personnel and maintenance during construction, were computed for Chandigarh, Rourkela, Durgapur, and Naya Nangal at Rs. 17,134, Rs. 21,250, Rs. 17,115, and Rs. 13,792 respectively. No less than 50 per cent of the developed land in these new towns remains for public or collective uses; their respective percentages are about 50, 53, 53, and 72 (Table 6). Development costs on public land uses must be apportioned among other land uses in order to calculate the per square foot rates. These rates are then applied to the average plot sizes for different housing types in order to calculate the related land and development costs.

For the four new towns of Chandigarh, Rourkela, Durgapur, and Naya Nangal, the land and development costs range between 17-36 per cent of construction costs of residential building (Table 25). Using 10 per cent of construction cost as a representative cost for land and development, therefore, leads to an underestimation of the base on which the economic rent is calculated. Furthermore, this relationship varies widely not only for towns but for different categories of housing. The percentage usually is lower for government employees getting monthly salaries under Rs. 200 and substantially higher for the higher salaried personnel.

The economic rent, social rent (the rent charged), and subsidy for different categories of housing for the government employees at Chandigarh, Rourkela, Durgapur, and Naya Nangal are presented in Table 26. The economic rent, and thus the subsidy, has been calculated at 8.5 per cent of the capital cost. The monthly economic rent per residential unit averages Rs. 71, 67, 88, and 54 respectively for Chandigarh, Rourkela, Durgapur, and Naya Nangal. The average rent charged is Rs. 17 at Chandigarh and Rs. 18.50 in the three industrial towns. Thus, the average monthly subsidy per dwelling unit or per government employee living in public housing ranges from Rs. 35.50 at Naya Nangal to Rs. 69.50 at Durgapur. Or the social rent is 21-34 per cent and the housing subsidy is 66-79 per cent of the economic rent. And each public employee lives in a subsidized house. The amount of

TABLE 25

Land and Development Costs as a Percentage of Construction
Costs for Different Categories of Housing at Chandigarh,
Rourkela, Durgapur and Naya Nangal

Monthly Salary	Chandigarh[a]	Rourkela Up to Second Phase	Durgapur Up to Second Phase	Naya Nangal
50-110	16	34	18	17
111-200	9	43	24	18
201-400	10) 9)	36	33	24
401-850	14	33	39	32
851-1,600	23) 24)	47	36	57
1,601-2,500	43) 42)	50	30	59
Special--Over Rs. 2,500	39	25	19	53
Average--All Categories	17	36	28	21

[a] Income categories for Chandigarh are slightly different. For details see Appendix D, Table 1.

Source: Based on data collected by the author.

TABLE 26

Economic Rent, Rent Charged and Subsidy for Different Categories of
Housing for Government Employees at Chandigarh, Rourkela, Durgapur
and Naya Nangal--Economic Rent 8.5 Per Cent of Capital Cost

Monthly Income Rs.	Monthly Economic $_a$ Rent--Rs.	Monthly Rent Charged Rs.	Monthly Subsidy Rs.	4 as % of 2	3 as % of 2	2 as % of 1
1	2	3	4	5	6	7
Chandigarh						
50-100	50.00	7.50	42.50	85	15	67
101-175	83.00	13.80	69.20	83	17	60
176-250	102.00	21.30	80.70	79	21	48
251-500	150.00	37.50	112.50	75	25	40
501-750	205.00	62.50	142.50	70	30	33
751-1,000	277.00	87.50	189.50	68	32	32
1,001-1,500	398.00	125.00	273.00	69	31	32
1,501-2,000	517.00	175.00	342.00	66	34	30
2,001-2,500	560.00	225.00	335.00	60	40	25
Special--over 2,500	1,078.00	250.00	828.00	77	23	43
Average Per Dwelling Unit	71.00	17.00	54.00	76	24	42
Rourkela--Up to Second Phase						
50-110	30.00	8.00	22.00	73	27	38
111-200	51.00	15.50	35.50	70	30	33
201-400	71.00	30.00	41.00	58	42	24
401-850	154.00	62.50	91.50	59	41	25
851-1,600	258.00	122.50	135.50	52	48	21
1,601-2,500	383.00	205.00	178.00	46	54	19
Special--over 2,500	766.00	250.00	516.00	67	33	31
Average Per Dwelling Unit	67.00	18.50	48.50	72	28	36

TABLE 26 — Continued

1	2	3	4	5	6	7
Durgapur--Up to Second Phase						
50-110	44.00	8.00	36.00	82	18	55
111-200	71.00	15.50	55.50	78	22	46
201-400	109.00	30.00	79.00	72	28	36
401-850	162.00	62.50	99.50	61	39	26
851-1,600	258.00	122.50	135.50	53	47	21
1,601-2,500	497.00	205.00	292.00	59	41	25
Special--over 2,500	836.00	250.00	586.00	70	30	33
Average Per Dwelling Unit	88.00	18.50	69.50	79	21	48
Naya Nangal						
50-110	34.00	8.00	26.00	76	24	43
111-200	65.00	15.50	49.40	76	24	42
201-400	103.00	30.00	73.00	71	39	34
401-850	164.00	62.50	101.50	62	38	26
851-1,600	272.00	122.50	149.50	55	45	22
1,601-2,500	349.00	205.00	144.00	41	59	17
Special--over 2,500	399.00	250.00	149.00	37	63	16
Average Per Dwelling Unit	54.00	18.50	35.50	66	34	29

[a]For details see Appendix D, Tables 1-4.

Source: Based on data collected by the author.

ubsidy, in absolute terms, increases with the increase in salary
f the government servant. The subsidy for the highest paid pub-
ic official may be as high as twenty times the subsidy for the
owest paid civil servant.

According to the earlier mentioned Finance Ministry's
Memoranda, the average subsidy for 100 houses should not exceed Rs. 1,500 per month or Rs. 2,625 when the cost of construction index at a particular location is 25 per cent higher than
n Delhi; it also provides that housing for government employees
receiving a monthly salary of above Rs. 300 should not normally
be subsidized. Table 24 shows, however, that in these three industrial towns, the monthly subsidy per 100 houses is Rs. 3,550
at Naya Nangal, Rs. 4,850 at Rourkela, and Rs. 6,950 at Durgapur. Not only do employees who draw salaries above Rs. 300
per month live in subsidized housing, but they also receive
larger subsidies than their counterparts in lower salary groups.
These figures represent an economic rent of 8.5 per cent of the
capital cost of residential buildings. When a 10 per cent rate is
applied, the subsidy for 100 houses amounts to Rs. 6,600 at
Chandigarh, Rs. 6,050 at Rourkela, Rs. 8,550 at Durgapur, and
Rs. 4,550 at the Fertilizer Corporation's town at Naya Nangal.
This information is represented graphically in Figures 2 and 3.

Is 10 per cent of the salary of the government employee a
reasonable charge for housing provided to him? One would expect that families within the lower and higher income groups
would spend a smaller proportion of their incomes on housing
than do middle-income families. Low-income families must
spend a major portion of their incomes on food so that little remains for shelter and other necessary items. They are forced
to live under substandard conditions--the main reason for sub-
sidizing their housing. The middle-income families also have a
smaller margin for housing than the highest income groups.
Most of them are white collar and professional workers whose
values often result in higher outlays of income on housing. The
elite presumably spend a lower proportion of their income on
housing. Therefore, there can be no justifiable reason for applying the 10 per cent rule to all categories of government employees. It would be logical to subsidize low-income housing,
but charge the rest the economic rent.

Housing subsidy for government employees is inequitable
in another way. Public housing is not provided to all government
employees. In industrial project towns, the percentage of the
employees provided with housing may be as low as the 13 per

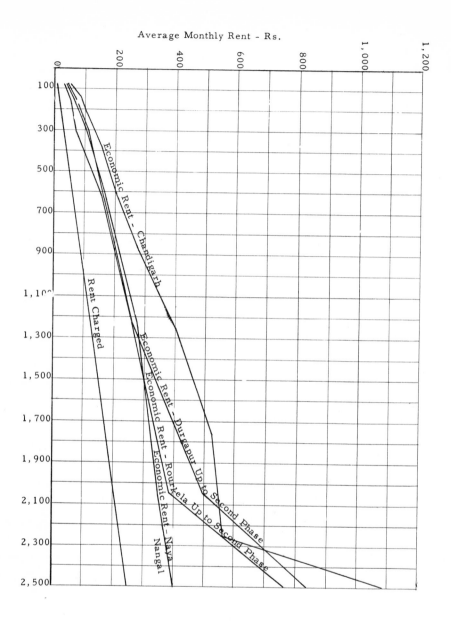

Average Monthly Rent - Rs.

Average Monthly Income - Rs.

Figure 2.   Monthly Economic Rent, Rent Charged and Subsidy for Different Categories of Government Employees' Housing in the
Four New Towns (Annual Economic Rent Calculated at 8.5
per cent of Capital Cost).

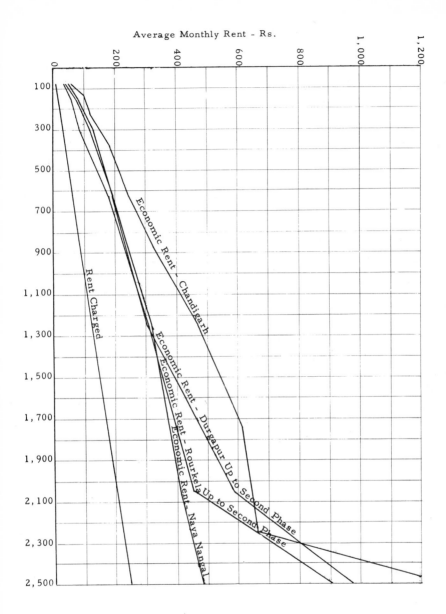

Average Monthly Rent - Rs.

Average Monthly Income - Rs.

Figure 3. Monthly Economic Rent, Rent Charged and Subsidy for Different Categories of Government Employees' Housing in the Four New Towns (Annual Economic Rent Calculated at 10 per cent of Capital Cost).

cent at the Hindustan Aircraft Limited Town at Bangalore. Usually, the percentage is lower when the new town is located near an existing urban area and higher when rural areas surround it. To illustrate: A and B each draw a salary of Rs. 300 per month; A has been provided with housing and B lives in the nearby town; both are located at new town X, where the per unit cost of housing for their salary group is Rs. 10,000. The annual economic rent for a house would then be 10 per cent of Rs. 10,000 or Rs. 1,000 or a monthly economic rent of Rs. 83.33. A would be paying Rs. 30 per month as rent, and his real income would be Rs. 353.33 (or Rs. 270 cash plus the use of the dwelling whose economic rent is Rs. 83.33). When B, living in a nearby town, rents a similar house, he pays at least Rs. 83.33 per month for it. His real income is still only his salary, Rs. 300 (or Rs. 216.67 plus the use of the dwelling). Therefore, A has the use of Rs. 53.33 more per month than B, or a real income about 18 per cent higher. B may be required to incur additional economic and social costs because of increased transportation and other related costs.

Alternative means of housing subsidy must be considered. Perhaps economic rent could be charged for all categories of housing, and the eligible low-income government employees might be given a special housing allowance in addition to their salaries as long as they lived in public housing when such housing is available. The amount of subsidy, then, could be reduced gradually with a rise in the real incomes of this group.

GUIDING INDIAN URBAN DEVELOPMENT

Formulation of an Urbanization Policy

The magnitude of Indian urbanization and its associated problems offers a tremendous challenge for development planning. A national policy on urbanization should be formulated that explicitly recognizes the indivisible nature of the economic, social, and physical aspects of the unparalleled growth of the urban population in the past as well as in the future. It is fallacious to regard urban growth as unnecessary and evil, and it is naive to desire and to expect that the urbanization trend can be halted or reversed. Developmental policies in India must bridge the gap between what is considered desirable and what is feasible.

The spatial consequences of the economic decisions necessary to implement the national plans have not been given sufficient consideration in the Five Year Plans by the Government of India. This may be seen in the lack of clearly defined Plan objectives and targets for the local and regional distribution of urbanization. Urbanization problems are treated in a fragmentary fashion, and to identify the public policy on them, one has to refer to the discussion in the Second and the Third Plans on such questions as industrial location, housing, slum clearance, and water development.

The development design of the national plans should be evolved only after thorough study and analysis of the functional importance and interdependence of different sized population centers. The tendency to dichotomize "rural" and "urban" must be replaced by the recognition of a continuum or rural-urban activities. The Report by the International Perspective Planning Team on Small Industries suggests a seven-tier classification of

population centers, indicating the major socio-economic functions that each typical center performs.[1] According to this hier-
archical arrangement, the metropolises perform the most com-
plex functions as super-regional centers of national and international importance, while the smallest villages of under 5,000
population, perform the most simple agricultural and traditional
village industrial functions. Studies on economies of scale and
agglomerative motives, as well as costs and revenues associated
with alternative patterns of urbanization, provide invaluable information based on the formulation of an urbanization policy.

In establishing goals and targets for urban development, the
national policy must necessarily be broad. It has been pointed
out that "regional planning is generally considered the level at
which national development goals, targets and policies can be
best given their spatial dimension and related to physical plans
at the local level."[2] The regional framework in turn should contribute to the formulation of national urbanization policy, and the
planning procedures "must be conceived as a two-way avenue al-
lowing for a continuous flow of information, consultation and ad-
vice between these two levels of planning."[3]

Urbanization policy should determine the appropriate regional and national levels of urbanization as an integral part of
national developmental strategy as well as those for specific plan
periods. It must select a pattern of urbanization based on a
broad benefit-cost analysis, and devise programs to facilitate
both inter- and intra-regional migration to achieve these objectives.

Because of the scarcity of resources for investment and
the high degree of capital intensiveness associated with investment in infra-structure, it is crucial that urban development
programs should aim for maximum utilization of the social overheads in existing urban centers. While some elements of infrastructure in Indian cities may be operating below capacity, in
others, capacity may be limited. These latter must therefore be

---

[1]The International Perspective Planning Team on Small
Industries, op. cit., p. 126.

[2]Leo Jakobson, op. cit., p. 60.

[3]Ibid., p. 60.

given higher priorities for investment to ensure maximum return on the overall cumulative investment in social overheads. Substantial investment has been made during the fifties and sixties in the development of new towns. In these towns excessive capacity exists due to the unrealistically high standards at which urban facilities were planned for such towns, and it may be desirable to further develop some of them as continuing growth nodes for future development.

Once the desirable degree and pattern of urbanization has been determined, the overall policies must be translated into workable programs for urban development. Components of the urban development program have been treated in the National Plans in a fragmented fashion. But such programs: urban land development; water supply, sewerage, and drainage; mass transit and transportation; housing, slum clearance, and redevelopment; open space recreation--all need to be coordinated into a single program for urban development.

A Budget for Urbanization

The implementation of any public policy depends, to a very large extent, upon the appropriate financial or budgetary provisions. Effectuation of urban development policies requires large investments in all social and economic overheads. As public investment planning is primarily guided by the National Plans, it is essential that the Five Year Plans include financial provision for urban development programs. Estimates of capital outlays may be integrated with the physical inputs of the many programs necessary to achieve the targets and goals of the stated policy. A tentative approach to investment planning for urban development is therefore outlined in the following paragraphs.

The most important goal of economic development is the increase of both the real income and the standard of living of the people within a particular country. Crucial variables in the formula for development are: an increase in the rate of savings and investment, and the improvement of the productivity of capital. The size of the total investment during any particular plan period is determined on the basis of the relationship between projections of national income and marginal capital-output and marginal saving-income ratios. Each development plan includes either explicitly or implicitly projections of national income cor-responding to the particular plan periods. Distribution of this income between the rural and the urban areas becomes critical.

Economic capacity to support urban development programs may be derived from the estimates of urban incomes during par-ticular plan periods. The ratio between this capacity and urban incomes may be derived by analyzing past trends in this rela-tionship, and depending upon the expected rate of economic growth, a higher percentage of income may be assumed to be available for future urban development. This is justifiable since the demand for public goods and services increases faster than the rise in real incomes and standards of living. In addition, a somewhat higher percentage of income for urban development during subsequent plan periods would be anti-inflationary and promote capital formation. Income available for urban programs is derived from local taxes, municipal utility prices, fees and fines, and that portion of state and federal levies which may be returned to the local governments under intergovernmental finan-cial arrangements.

It has been shown that the relationship between capital costs and annual maintenance and operating costs may be deter-mined and expressed as ratios between the two. These ratios differ for alternative patterns of urbanization as well as for sep-arate components of the total program. It is necessary, there-fore, to develop a weighted average ratio, or ratios, that take into account capital/annual cost relationship for different elem-ents of the urban development program.

Multiplying the amount representing economic capacity by the average ratio between capital and annual costs, we calculate the total capital investment in urban development programs com-mensurate with the projected economy during the next plan per-iod. By deducting from this total figure the depreciation value of the existing investment in the ongoing programs, the net invest-ment or an urbanization budget may be determined. This budget figure serves as a financial constraint in the determination of standards as well as levels at which programs may be pursued. It is an invaluable informational base when evaluating alter-natives, assigning priorities, and phasing different programs, as well as in the formulation of local taxation policies, and pol-icies for intergovernmental financial relations.

Land Policy for Urban Development

There is no way to expand the total land on the surface of the earth. The per capita availability of land is less in India than in many other countries.[4] The land-man ratio has been declining in India because of the increasing population--in 1900 3.4 acres of land were available per person in India compared to 1.8 acres in 1960. Population projections for 1971 and 1981 predict that this ratio may decline to 1.44 and 1.16 respectively.

In theory, the supply of land for urban uses is limited only by the total supply of land. "For the most part the cities grow by absorbing farm lands."[5] These additions in any particular area are determined by the relationship between agricultural and urban land values. "The urban use must create a land value just higher than the farm value to induce a shift from one use to another. Of course, urban land values may and do rise much higher than farm values."[6] Although land for urban uses is available so long as urban land values exceed agricultural land value, there are competing demands on it for rural use. Furthermore, any parcel of land in an urban or a rural area is capable of many uses. "Like every rational economic choice, the determination of the most appropriate land use is an extremely vital social decision."[7]

The national as well as the state governments in India recognize the importance of an appropriate land policy for urban development. Chapter XXXIII of the Third Five Year Plan on

---

[4] The per capita land area in India today is 1.8 acres, as compared to 181.9 acres in Australia, 26.5 acres in the U.S.S.R., 12.8 acres in the United States, 9.9 acres in Burma, 4.9 acres in Communist China, and 2.5 acres in Pakistan and Poland.

[5] Richard U. Ratcliff, Real Estate Analysis (New York: McGraw-Hill Book Company, Inc., 1961), p. 44.

[6] Ibid., p. 44.

[7] India (Republic), Ministry of Health, "Note on Urban Land Policy," Proceedings of the Second Conference of State Ministers for Town and Country Planning (Trivandrum: October 13-15, 1961), p. 195.

"Housing and Urban and Rural Planning" devotes a separate section to Urban Planning and Land Policy. "[8] The following measures are suggested in order to reduce the high cost of urbanization:

1. Control of urban land values through public acquisition of land and appropriate fiscal policies;

2. Physical planning of the use of land and the preparation of master plans;

3. Defining tolerable minimum standards for housing and other services to be provided for towns according maximum standards to the extent necessary; and,

4. Strengthening of municipal administrations for undertaking new development responsibilities. [9]

The emphasis is upon achieving planned uses of urban land through preparation of physical master plans, and curbing speculation and holding down land prices by large-scale public acquisition of land in advance, by freezing urban land values, and by limiting the compensation liability for land that may be acquired.

---

[8]Ibid., p. 679-99. The Committee on Urban Land Policy, appointed by a resolution passed at a Joint Session of the Central Council of Local Self-Government and the State Ministers for Town Planning held at New Delhi in September 1963, adopted the four principle social objectives of urban land policy: (1) to achieve an optimum social use of urban land; (2) to make land available in adequate quantity, at the right time and for reasonable prices to both the public and private authorities and individuals; (3) to encourage cooperative community effort and bonafide individual builders in the field of land development, housing, and construction; and (4) to prevent concentration of land ownership in a few private hands and safeguard specially the interest of the poor and underprivileged sections of urban society. See India (Republic), Ministry of Health, "Report of the Committee on Urban Land Policy" (New Delhi: 1964), pp. 14-15. (Mimeographed.)

[9]The Third Five Year Plan, p. 690.

The goals conceived by the Planning Commission and the Committee on Urban Land Policy are worth striving for. The means they suggest to achieve these objectives suffer from two major shortcomings. The role of the market as a disciplined, self-adjusting mechanism is more or less ignored, and the inter-relationships between rural and urban land taxation systems, compensation policy and selling and/or leasing of urban land have not been given serious consideration. The Committee on Urban Land Policy feels that the market value of land in urban areas is higher than its actual worth since market prices reflect unearned increments in land values as well as potential development value. Payment of compensation to owners whose land may be acquired is unfair to public authorities and to the community which has to bear the financial burden of such compensation costs through taxes and other charges. In order to limit the compensation liability for land acquisition two measures are suggested: ante-dating compensation or freezing land values, [10] and advance acquisition of land.

It is logical that the Planning Commission, the Town and Country Planning Organization, and the Committee on Urban Land Policy show concern for high land prices in urban areas; but to limit the compensation liability as suggested by them raises certain crucial constitutional, administrative, and economic questions. The implications of these important issues have been clouded by ideological considerations. When solutions to economic problems are sought through non-economic methods they are unlikely to be acceptable to society as a whole.

Government in any country is based on the implied assent of its members that the individual private interest shall be subservient to the public interest. The private interest is subordinate to the common welfare of the country as a whole. Necessitas publica major est quam privata. The power of "Eminent Domain" or public acquisition of land is inherent in every governmental system. Except in the totalitarian countries--where such power

_____

[10]The Town and Country Planning Organization in their Draft Model Act for Acquisition of Land for Town Planning Purposes recommends that amount of compensation shall be the equivalent of the market value of land as of January 1, 1951, plus 25 per cent of the difference between market value of land at the date of publication of the notification for acquisition and the market value on January 1, 1951.

may be confiscatory--this right of the State to appropriate private property for public purpose must provide for just compensation to the persons for the loss of their properties. Article 31(2)
of the Constitution of India dealing with the question of compensation for public acquisition of land does not qualify the word
"compensation" by the word "just." The Supreme Court of India
in State of West Bengal v. Bela Banerjee upheld the word "compensation" as meaning a "full and fair money equivalent" of the
property taken and any law which denies this must be held to be
void."[11] In another case the Supreme Court declared that "...
the provision for compensation is merely a cloak for confiscat-
ory legislation. It is not open to the Legislature to lay down any
principles which may result in nonpayment of compensation or
which may result in not paying any compensation whatsoever."[12]

Because of Court decisions unfavorable to the government,
Article 31(2) was amended in 1955.[13] According to Durga Das
Basu, "This change is the result of the reaction to the decision in
the case of Bela Banerjee to the effect that under the existing cl.
(2), the Court had jurisdiction to enquire in every case of appro-
priation of private property by the State whether the person ap-
propriated has been ensured the true value of the property ap-
propriated."[14] The amended clause (2) of Article 31 reads:

> No property shall be compulsorily acquired or re-
> quisitioned save for a public purpose and save by au-
> thority of a law which provides for compensation for
> the property so acquired or requisitioned and either
> fixes the amount of the compensation or specifies the
> compensation is to be determined and given; and no
> such law shall be called in question in any court on
> the ground that the compensation provided by that law
> is not adequate.[15]

---

[11] State of West Bengal v. Bela Banerjee (1954), Supreme
Court Appeals, 41(45).

[12] State of Bihar v. Kameshwar, All India Reports (1952),
Supreme Court Appeals, 252.

[13] The Constitution (Fourth Amendment) Act, 1955.

[14] Durga Das Basu, Commentary on Constitution of India
(Calcutta: S. C. Sarkar & Sons Ltd., 1955, Third Edition, Volume 1), p. 833.

[15] The Constitution (Fourth Amendment) Act, 1955.

Under the Fourth Amendment the question of "adequacy" of compensation has been taken from the Courts; the final judgment is with the Legislature. Basu feels that "Though it is extremely risky to hazard any opinion as to what view the Supreme Court will take as to the interpretation of the word 'adequate,' it would be wrong to suppose that all questions relating to the exercise of the power of eminent domain have been taken away from the jurisdiction of the Courts."[16] He further points out that:

> Of course, the amended cl. (2) says that the 'adequacy of compensation' shall not be justifiable, but, according to canons of legal construction, this provision cannot be used to control independent provisions outside Art. 31(2). Thus, a law providing for 'deprivation,' 'acquisition' or 'requisition' shall still be open to be challenged on the ground that it offends against Art. 14.[17]

Even if ante-dating or freezing of land values for compensation purposes were constitutionally permissible, it would be grossly inequitable unless all land was nationalized. The persons whose lands were acquired would be more disadvantaged than those whose land would continue to remain in private ownership. If large tracts of land were notified for simultaneous acquisition, the consistent upward trend in urban land market values would cause an increasing inequity in compensation at successive stages of the acquisition process in particular urban areas. Obviously all notifications could not be made at once, but would be stretched out over thirty or forty years, and possession of and compensation for lands covered by a single notification would be spread over several years.

Determination of compensation for public acquisition of land, if related to market value at some previous date, would create other very real administrative difficulties. Most of the land acquisition cases referred to the Courts under Section 18 of the Land Acquisition Act, 1894, pertain to compensation. These cases contest that the amount of compensation awarded by the

---

[16] Durga Das Basu, op. cit., p. 835.

[17] Ibid., p. 835. Article 14, concerned with the Right to Equality provides that "The State shall not deny to any person equality before the law or the equal protection of the laws within the territory of India."

Collector was different from the market value of the land on the date of notification under Section 4. The acquisition process in the absence of an intervention by a Court of Law may take about two years.[18] When a Court intervenes the process is much longer. Because determination of compensation from a predated market value is inequitable, it naturally increases the incidence of Court cases and prolongs the acquisition process. As success of an urban land policy largely depends upon the speed at which the acquisition process proceeds, the lengthening of the process frustrates its objectives.

An urban land policy may function both as a planning device for guiding future development and as a resource for financing such development. Acquisition of land by public authorities is one means of achieving rational land use according to plan, but public ownership must not become an end in itself. Development and disposal of urban land are vital concerns of public policy which must also deal with such questions as the type of development to be carried out before disposal by public agencies. the leasing or selling of the land, and the appropriate pricing policies for land disposal.

The effectiveness of the measures for achieving objectives of land policy largely depend upon the relationship of these measures to the system of taxation of urban and urbanizable land. The present system of taxation of real estate is not entirely satisfactory for urban development, and certain modifications are necessary. The following changes are minimal:

1. Change-over of the basis of assessment for taxation of land and buildings from the annual rental to capital (market) value.

2. Separation of assessments for land and improvements.

3. State valuation organizations for assessment of land and buildings for the purposes of municipal taxation.

4. A tax levied on transfer of properties.

---

[18]The Law Commission of India, as quoted in Note on Urban Land Policy, op. cit., p. 215.

These changes would make the system of real estate taxation more equitable and more productive; they would discourage speculation in land, encourage building activity, and promote more efficient and economic uses of land; they would tax the unearned increment in land values and in all likelihood result in a reduction of the market price of land.

An Approach to Integrated Physical and Financial Planning

In India, it has been noted that urban planning in general and planning for the new towns in particular has been based on predetermined land use and functional standards, and that financial planning and budgeting have not been integrated into the planning processes at local levels. Ad hoc standards have been the most important determinants of financial decision-making in the planning and development of new towns. In one sense, the master plan itself becomes "a type of standard, combining both programmatic and land use standards,"[19] and precludes any systematic consideration of alternative patterns or programs for development. More seriously, the community's economic well being (for economic capacity) is completely neglected.

Physical and financial planning are integral parts of the effective decision-making process for urban and regional development. Financial planning is concerned with determining the overall level of capital outlays (investments) establishing priorities among different programs and activities, estimating, allocating, and rationing funds and other resources, and relating the capital improvement programs to the budgetary processes of the governmental units concerned. Financial planning as a decision-making process also deals with both long- and short-term revenue and expenditure programs.

Public investment planning for urban development involves three different but related types of decision-making operations: determining the overall level of capital outlays, assigning priorities and allocating resources for different programmatic needs, and coordinating these with the budgetary processes of the governmental units responsible for urban development. Not implied is a clear-cut separation of functional responsibilities in the

---

[19]Brown and Gilbert, op. cit., pp. 282-83.

planning process. Each operation involves overlapping but differing time horizons -- determination of the overall capital requirements may take longer than the five or six years required for the other operations. To some extent, the inputs and outputs of the three sets of operations also vary. These operations, however, involve constant feedback and must be viewed as equally important components of the total planning process.

I have outlined elsewhere an approach to the development of a theoretical framework in which physical, programmatic, and financial aspects are considered essential components of the planning process.[20] Briefly, the preparation of a long-term plan takes into account: alternative programmatic and land use needs derived from the urban development goals and from functional standards; capital costs associated with the above programs; estimated annual maintenance and operating costs (interest, depreciation, and operating expenditures) during the expected life of the proposed facilities; intergovernmental revenues; community responsibility; and the community's economic capacity expressed as a proportion of the estimated or projected income for the area. Financial planning is a continuous process, and the interaction among the above variables is conceived as iterating until the community's responsibility (i.e., annual maintenance and operating costs minus intergovernmental revenues) approximates its economic capacity. This process is then coordinated with the governmental budgetary process, which treats the capital and the operating budgets as parts of one process.

Summary

Major changes are considered essential in India's public policy on urban and regional development. The need for coordination between spatial and economic aspects of developmental

---

[20]Ved Prakash, op. cit., pp. 206-33. See also "A Framework for Planning-Programming-Budgeting System for Local Governments, " a paper presented at the 1967 National Conference of the American Society for Public Administration, San Francisco, March 27-30, 1967.

planning is apparent and each of the Five Year Plans should incorporate a budget for urban development. In order to facilitate implementation of a public policy concerning urban development at local and regional levels, the adoption of suitable land policies are assigned crucial importance. Finally, an approach to integrated physical and financial planning for individual urban areas must be adopted which would facilitate the improvement of planning standards as well as provide an appropriate framework and generate suitable information for budgetary-decision-making.

CHAPTER VI

IMPLICATIONS OF NEW TOWN DEVELOPMENT

India's urban population of 27 million in 1900 had, by 1961, almost trebled. During these sixty years, the urban population, as a per cent of the total population, increased from about twelve to eighteen. The largest cities and metropolitan areas (with populations of 100,000 and over) had the highest rate of growth among the six Census classes into which the urban areas are divided. Of the urban area increment of 17 million persons during 1951-61, more than 11 million were added to the cities of over 100,000 population.

An important objective of the Five Year Plans is balanced growth among different regions by the promotion of geographic dispersal of industrial and economic activities. Because rural development and urbanization are complementary, they must not be viewed as necessarily in conflict. However, the intellectual and political climate in India is anti-urban in outlook, especially against the larger urban centers, and there appears to be a built-in bias in favor of building and preserving self-sustaining small communities. Public policies aimed at decentralized industrial development stem from this conflict and call for smaller and medium-sized urban areas, the decongestion of very large cities, the limitation to certain sizes of the growth of other urban areas, and the establishment of new towns.

New Towns in India--An Evaluation

Since 1947 more than thirty new towns have been planned and constructed in India. Most of these towns have been built by public corporations in conjunction with industrial projects. The new town idea has great appeal to the industrial corporations

within the public sector since most of the projects under construction include the building of separate new towns for corporate
staff and employees. Pursuant to the goal of a "socialist pattern
of society," enlargement of the public sector is to be increasingly
expected. Therefore, under the present public policy framework,
the establishment of more industrial towns may proceed with
even greater vigor. So far the role played by the new towns in
the urbanization process has been insignificant while the population has grown fastest in the largest cities and metropolitan areas
during the 1951-61 decade.

New Towns and Urban Development

The alternate paths which Indian urbanization may travel
during the rest of the twentieth century need careful reexamin-
ation. The questions of costs and methods of financing, of economies of scale, of localization, and of urbanization must be considered. It is likely that smaller urban areas do not offer these
economies and would, on analysis, prove unattractive for the location and expansion of economic activities. The study by the International Perspective Team on Small Industries points out that
in the recent past even the small-scale factories and industrial
estates have developed more rapidly in larger, more industrially
advanced urban areas. It might have been preferable to create
suitable opportunities for sustained economic growth in these
towns and cities by a phased program of investment in economic
and social overheads and by the location of manufacturing industries. Most of them, now, have little or no manufacturing industries, and little infrastructure and other public facilities. Therefore, the new towns can be justified only when comparative cost
calculations indicate definite advantages.

Most of the new towns were originally planned as single-
purpose communities, in fact, one-industry towns. Furthermore,
industrial locations were decided without giving serious consideration to the locational interdependence of different economic
activities at particular locations. Where one or more industrial
projects have subsequently been located contiguous to the boundaries of the initial project, coordination between planning and
development of these areas is the exception rather than the rule.

Since the new towns were conceived as single-industry
communities, the location of the industry and the planning and

development of the municipal services, housing, and other community facilities were based on what may be called a project-type approach. Thus, even though it is of great importance that industrial location and site selection be based on industrial-complex analysis, the locational interdependence of activities was given very little serious consideration.

An urban community dependent upon a single-industry has a one-sided economic base. The large-scale industrial plants on which the new towns are dependent are presently operating in virtual isolation of both the urban and the regional environment around them. To the extent that artificial barriers exist, a different conglomeration of economic activities and the creation of an umbrella of operating utilities, such as those advocated by Harris as essential for future development, will be slow to develop in such new towns. Furthermore, at times in the past, single industry towns have proven to be highly unstable during the downward swing of economic cycles. [1]

The lack of coordination between physical planning and economic setting is evident in most of the industrial new towns. The steel town at Bhilai has been planned for 100,000. The number of employees, as of March 1, 1964, was 24,570. The capacity of the Bhilai Steel Plant is now being expanded from one million tons to two and a half million tons of ingot steel per annum. The expansion was expected to have been completed by March 1966, and the number of employees was expected to be 29,322. Assuming that the average number of dependents per employee is four, the population on April 1, 1966, was to be 146,000 or about 46 per cent more than the population for which the municipal services were planned under the master plan. This situation probably is repeated in other industrial towns.

New Towns and the Non-Project Population. The most serious failure of the town plans, however, is the inadequate provision of space and municipal facilities for the non-project employees or the supporting population. The project employees live in clean new homes, generally with individual gardens; their children go to modern schools; their hospitals have the latest

---

[1] See Ira M. Robinson, New Industrial Towns on Canada's Resource Frontier (Chicago, Illinois: Department of Geography, University of Chicago, 1962), Chapter VI, "Economic Base," pp. 91-103.

equipment and furnishings; and in the evenings the project population can go to clubs--there are separate clubs for officers and workers. The employees and their families live what some call the "good life." However, such basic urban amenities as stores, repair shops, and movie theaters, are either inadequate or non-existent within the planned towns. Therefore, these facilities have sprung up either on the outskirts of the planned towns or in the adjoining areas. Their supporting population are denied the facilities provided within the new towns, and must live in shanty towns and slums, without water supply and sewerage facilities; only the stores may have electricity. Thus "old" and new town patterns develop side-by-side. Economically, and to some extent socially, both are parts of one functional system. If due to extreme overcrowding and lack of basic public health facilities, an epidemic disease were to break out in the adjoining areas, it would also affect adversely the health of the residents within the planned new towns.

New Town Administration

The management of the public corporations responsible for development within the new towns, does not feel any real concern for development beyond the town boundaries and these new towns are, in a sense, walled industrial cities; nor does it favor unified created separate local self-governments in some of the industrial towns. The area of a new town is notified and a notified area committee is constituted.[2] The Notified Area Committee for the steel town at Rourkela was constituted by the State Government of Orissa,[3] and consists of twelve members, each designated by

---

[2] A notified area committee is one form of local government in India which is less autonomous than the municipalities and the municipal corporations. The members of the notified area committee are nominated by the state governments concerned. These committees formulate the by-laws which must be approved by the respective state governments before they can become effective. Generally speaking, these committees are granted lesser tax and other revenue powers than the other municipal bodies in urban areas.

[3] Government of Orissa, Health (L. S. G.) Department, Notification No. 6191-LSG dated June 17, 1963, published in an extraordinary issue of the Orissa Gazette No. 427 dated June 19, 1963.

the office held either in the Steel Project or the State Government. The Town Administrator of Hindustan Steel Limited is the Chairman of the Committee, of which eight members are employees of the steel project, and the other three are the Superintendent of Police, the Development Officer, and the Sub-Divisional Officer of the subdivision of the State in which the steel plant is located. Thus it is not a representative body of the community.

The Committee on Plan Projects suggested a special type of legislation for industrial towns under which the administration of these towns would be left to the separate, notified area committees. The Committee felt that the administration of industrial towns should rest fully with the industrial authority as defense authorities have effective control in military cantonments.[4]

Do the attitudes of the public corporation and the recommendations made by the Committee on Plan Projects relate to the "balanced regional development" and "rural-urban integration" policies stated in the Five Year Plans and other public policy statements mentioned earlier? Unfortunately, the new towns policy violates the overall public policy for socio-economic development in India. It is hard to reconcile the building of walled industrial cities with a concern for the development of associated regiona.

The new towns associated with public sector industrial projects have far-reaching social implications. It is natural for the non-employee population to be jealous of the project employees because of the vast differences in the level of municipal services and housing which each group enjoys. Many of the employees and their families are enjoying luxury for the first time in these surroundings, and during the initial stages, company paternalism may be accepted without resentment. But the report on Single-enterprise Communities in Canada points out:

> ...the combination of roles of employer, landlord, chief taxpayer, store operator, and local government inevitably leads to difficult social relationships between the company officials and the townspeople in a single-enterprise community. When the company engages in activities other than its industrial processes, the usual economic relationships between employer and employees become complicated.

---

[4] The Committee on Plan Projects, op. cit., pp. 64-66.

In the single-enterprise communities, 'industrial relations' become 'community relations' because the
company must now deal with not only its employees
but with the employees' wives and children. In these
circumstances the company is likely to take a pater-
nalistic attitude towards its employees and their dependents in an effort to make the community 'one big
happy family.' Unfortunately, the involvement of the
company in community and social affairs often cre-
ates additional difficulties.[5]

The situation is not very different at Jamshedpur--a company
town in the private sector.[6] In public sector company towns the
paternalism may not be dissimilar, since state paternalism is
substituted for private company paternalism.

If locational factors justify establishment of new industrial
centers, they could be planned as regional cities to serve as
growing points for regional development. Basic economic and
social overheads in adequate measure would provide suitable opportunities for the development of industrial complexes as well
as the service and the tertiary sectors. Whether we want it or
not, these new towns are going to be among the future metropolises of India. Planners in India must learn lessons from Western
experience with metropolitan problems. Multiplicity and frag-
mentation of local governments can still be avoided.

Costs and Revenues. Governmental capital costs, in the
new towns for which the data were available, average around Rs.
3,000 per capita. Of this amount, Rs. 627 represent land development costs--acquisition, survey, leveling, streets, sewerage,
and drainage are examples. Water supply and electricity distribution account for another Rs. 286. Per capita costs for government employees' housing are Rs. 1,943, and the balance is for
non-residential buildings.

[5]The Institute of Local Government, Queen's University,
Single-enterprise Communities in Canada, A Report to Central
Mortgage and Housing Corporation (Kingston: Queen's University, 1953), p. 223. See Chapter XV, "Social Problems," pp.
223-249.

[6]Unesco Research Center, Report on a Preliminary Inquiry
on the Growth of Steel Towns in India - A Study on Problems of
Urbanization (Calcutta: Unesco Research Center, 1959), 11. 92-95.

The per capita annual maintenance and operating costs have been estimated to be between Rs. 258 and Rs. 314--Rs. 50-63 for land developments, Rs. 43-57 for utilities, and Rs. 165-194 for housing.[7] Detailed information on maintenance and operating costs and revenues was not available except for Naya Nangal, where the per capita annual costs were found to be Rs. 496 for the year 1962-63. During the same year, per capita revenues were Rs. 79. The per capita deficit was thus Rs. 417.

The average per capita personal income in the three new industrial towns at Durgapur, Bhilai, and Naya Nangal has been computed to be about Rs. 450 in 1963-64. The annual maintenance and operating costs (Rs. 258-314) range between 57 to 70 per cent of the personal income of residents of these new towns. Therefore, the annual costs seem to be too high when related to the ability to pay.

Investment in housing for public employees accounts for more than half of the total governmental costs for developing the new towns. The average per capita capital costs are Rs. 1, 943, whereas the per capita estimated annual maintenance and operating costs range between Rs. 165 and Rs. 194 in the four new towns--Chandigarh, Rourkela, Durgapur and Naya Nangal--for which economic rent, rent charged, and subsidy have been analyzed in detail. It has been found that the average monthly subsidy per family, or per residential unit, ranges from Rs. 35.50 at Naya Nangal to Rs. 69.50 at Durgapur. The extent of subsidy is 66 per cent at Naya Nangal and 79 per cent at Durgapur of the economic rents. The present practice results in an under-estimation of costs for government employees' housing and understates the economic rent as well as the subsidy. The stated policy is not to subsidize housing for government employees drawing salaries over Rs. 3, 600 per year. However, housing for each and every government employee is subsidized, and the amount of subsidy generally increases with an increase in the salary of the public employee.

---

[7]These costs exclude operating expenditures for education, medical care and public health, but include depreciation and the interest on capital for building these facilities.

This study demonstrates that the cost of municipal and other urban facilities and of housing in the new towns are very high in comparison with the general level of incomes in these communities. These costs are much higher than some of the estimates made earlier by different authorities on the cost of urbanization in India.[8] High costs show that the land use and programmatic standards which form the basis of planning for most of the new towns are too high. The standards appear to be excessive even when the annual cost, as related to the economic capacity of the inhabitants of these communities, is projected for twenty or thirty years. Even if the inter-governmental revenues within the framework of existing public policies are taken into account, the new towns probably will not become self-supporting during the life-time of the presently built municipal and other facilities.

The main reason for the extravagant standards is that planning for the new towns is based on predetermined rather than rational investment criteria--economic analysis, rate of return analysis, or benefit-cost analysis. The Indian planners mainly concern themselves with the physical aspects of plan preparation for urban development. Urban planning in India also relies heavily on the concepts and techniques evolved during the nineteenth and the twentieth centuries in the West, particularly in the United States and Great Britain. The attempt is to transplant Western standards rather than to modify them to suit Indian conditions.

Physical and financial planning are integral parts of the planning process, and a lack of coordination between the two results in the adoption of unrealistic planning standards. The capital improvement programming and budgeting process is very rudimentary, and plays an insignificant role in decision-making

---

[8]Our analyses indicate the cost to be about Rs. 3,000 per capita. Pitambar Pant puts this figure at Rs. 1,950; Britton Harris at Rs. 600; and Catherine Bauer Wurster at Rs. 1,998. For details see: Pitambar Pant, "Urbanization and Long-Range Strategy," in Roy Turned (ed.), op. cit., p. 189; Britton Harris, "Centralization and Planned Development," op. cit., p. 265; and Catherine Bauer Wurster, "Overhead Costs and Development," in Roy Turner (ed.), op. cit., p. 297.

for investment planning in the development of new towns. Insuf ficient attention is paid to revenue programming. The benevol ence of public enterprises restricts the use of rigorous analyses and management tools justifiable on economic grounds. The theory and practice for administering public utilities can offer objective criteria for determining investment as well as pricing policies for such facilities. The framework for analyzing the new towns, developed in this study, and the approaches discussed for financial planning and for evolving suitable land policies for urban development, may prove to be of significant value.

Economists agree that widespread private conspicuous con sumption in developing nations is dysfunctional and is an impor tant deterrent to their economic growth. Some of the social re form measures, such as abolition of the dowry system in India, are aimed at dealing with this problem of conspicuous consump tion that can be defined as "lavish or wasteful spending regarded as establishing or enhancing social prestige."[9] It is reasonable to conclude that conspicuous consumption is rampant in the plan ning of new towns, and may very well embrace many of the other developmental schemes.

Excessive Standards and the Maintenance Problem

Scarcity of resources is a major constraint upon invest ment in municipal and other urban facilities that are crucial to the urbanization process. Once built, capital facilities need proper maintenance and entail recurring costs. Maintenance and operating costs vary, depending upon the degrees of capital in tensities associated with different programs. The need for prop er maintenance, however, is more crucial for facilities of lower quality and less critical for those of high quality, at least during the initial years.

Any judgment on the adequacy of maintenance of the new town facilities in the context of this study must necessarily be superficial and subjective in nature. Yet, during the field work

[9]Webster's Third New International Dictionary (Springfield, Massachusetts: G. & C. Merriam Company, 1961), p. 485.

stage the author spent some time in several of these communities and could not help but observe that such facilities as roads, buildings, parks, and recreation were in poor maintenance. Albert O. Hirschman alludes to the lack of proper maintenance of capital assets in the developing nations when he points out that

> This /lack of proper maintenance/ is perhaps one of the most characteristic failings of underdeveloped countries and one that is spread over the whole economic landscape. Eroding soils, stalled trucks, leaking roofs, prematurely run-down machines, unsafe bridges, clogged-up irrigation ditches--all testify to the same pervasive and paradoxical trait: the inadequate care for existing capital in capital-poor countries.[10]

The organizations responsible for management of the new town facilities must recognize maintenance as a special problem--more administrative or managerial than financial. They must be reoriented to exigencies of conditions created by the development of new facilities. Immediately after the Indo-China border conflict during the second half of 1962, governmental organizations embarked upon an economy drive. The maintenance budgets for different functions in the new industrial towns were arbitrarily modified by lowering customary percentage applied to the capital costs for estimating the current expenditures--allotment for maintenance of residential buildings, generally based on 2.5 per cent of capital cost of such buildings, was reduced by changing the percentage to 1.5. As a consequence, the interval between regular maintenance and repair was lengthened. Since maintenance and repair expenditures play a small part in the total annual maintenance and operating costs including depreciation and interest, the above reduction may be illusory for certain facilities because the depreciation will increase during the period of poor repair.

[10] Albert O. Hirschman, The Strategy of Economic Development (New Haven: Yale University Press, 1964), p. 141.

Conclusion

There is an urgent need to evaluate some alternate urbanization patterns in order to formulate appropriate objectives and targets for urban development commensurate with developmental goals and to reorient the new town policy in the context of these objectives; second, that it is essential to coordinate the various Five Year Plan schemes into a single program for urban development; and finally, that the economic growth models should incorporate suitable variables to allocate investment for urbanization corresponding to national plan periods.

QUESTIONNAIRE

Graduate School of Business and Public Administration
Cornell University, Ithaca, New York

FORD FOUNDATION
8 Rawdon Street, Calcutta - 16

FINANCING NEW TOWNS IN INDIA

BACKGROUND INFORMATION

Name of the town and its location.

Sponsoring Authority (Department and/or Ministry responsible for the establishment and development of the town).

Original purpose for which the town was established.

How and why was the present site selected?

Size of the town
Area
Population for which the town has been planned
Present population (or population in 1961)

Was a master/comprehensive plan prepared for the new town?

Who was responsible for the preparation of the plan? (Name of the agency, consultant, etc.)

When was the preparation of the master plan initiated?

When was the preparation of the plan completed?

ELEMENTS OF THE PLAN

What is the size of the planning area?

For what period was the plan prepared?

For what ultimate population was the town planned?

In how many planning districts/planning sectors/planning areas was the total planned area divided for the purposes of detailed planning? How was this division arrived at? What is the size of each planning-district/planning-area?

Land Use Analyses

Total Planned Area – Acres

Category	Planning District/Sector Number											
:	I :	II :	III :	IV :	V :	VI :	VII :	VIII :	IX :	X :	XI :	XII :
Residential												
Roads												
Educational												
Recreational												
Commercial												
Public and Semi-Public												
Industrial												
Vacant Land Buildable Unbuildable												
Peripheral Land												
Gross Sector Area												

What was the overall density planned for the new town? What densities were planned for different sectors and for various land uses?   (Housing Density-Neighborhood Density-Sector/District Density)

What were the standards for the following facilities or how were the land requirements for various functions determined?

a. Water   Gallons per capita per day
   - for residential areas
   - for industrial and other uses

b. Power

c. Schools   Within a walking distance of:
   - Nursery
   - Primary
   - Secondary

d. Recreation   Size and within a walking distance of:
   - Tot Lots
   - Children's Park
   - Adults' Playground
   - Adults' Park

e. Residential (per family)   Plinth Area   Plot Area
   - low income
   - middle income
   - upper income

f. Industrial   Per Worker

g. Health Center   Size and average walking distance

h. Groceries &
   Local Shopping   Size and average walking distance

i. Post Office   Size and average walking distance

j. Roads & Streets   Right-of-way   Length   No. of
                        (feet)   (miles)   Lanes
   1. Arterial Roads
   2. Major Roads
   3. Neighborhood Roads
   4. Residential Streets
   5. Others - Please specify

FINANCIAL ASPECTS

What was the overall estimated capital investment for the development of the new town?

What portion of the total costs was to be financed by the public sector?

Please give a break-down of the total costs (as phased for the following functions and programs):

Amount in Rupees

Function or Program	Total Estimated Capital Cost	First Five Years	Next Five Years	Rest of the Plan Period
Land Acquisition				
Development of Land				
Water Supply				
Drainage and Sewage Treatment				
Electricity (Power)				
Streets and Roads, etc.				
Type I (Specify)				
Type II (Specify)				
Type III (Specify)				
Schools				
Nursery				
Primary				
Secondary				
Hospitals				
Recreation				
Industry				
Commerce				
Housing				

How were the maintenance and operating costs for different functions and programs determined?

Please give annual maintenance and operating cost for all the programs:

	During the Construction Phase	After Completion of the Project (Specify Period)
1. Water Supply		
2. Power		
3. Sewerage and Drainage		
4. Streets and Roads - break-down for different types		
5. Public Buildings - please specify		
6. Lighting of Streets		
7. Parks and Playgrounds		
8. Regulation of Traffic		
9. Residential Buildings with break-up for different categories		
10. Other Public Facilities		
Total		

Which organizations were involved in providing resources for financing capital costs of different programs?

Please indicate the extent of their participation in the following table:

Particulars of the Organization	Function	Amount to be Provided with Dates	Whether Loan or Grant	If an Advance, How Was it to be Repaid?
A. International Organizations				
1. (Name)				
2.				
3.				
4.				
B. Central Government				
1. (Ministry)				
2.				
3.				
4.				
5.				
6.				
C. State Government				
1. (Department)				
2.				
3.				
4.				
5.				
D. Other Public Agencies				
1. (Specify)				
E. Private Sector				
1. (Name)				
2.				
F. Other Organizations				

Was there any other source from which capital financing was expected? If so, please specify the source and other relevant information on the lines of the above table.

Please give a summary of the total estimated capital costs and estimated resources for financing them.

What methods were envisaged for recouping the maintenance and operating costs in respect to different functions? Please supply this information in the following pro forma.

Functions/Program	Method of Recouping the Maintenance and Operating Costs
1. Public Utilities	
a. Water	
b. Electricity	
c. Sewerage and Drainage	
d. Street Lighting	
2. Streets, etc.	
3. Parks and Recreation	
4. Schools	
a. Nursery	
b. Primary	
c. Secondary	
5. Other Institutions	
a. Hospitals	
6. Others - Please Specify	

EXECUTION AND/OR IMPLEMENTATION OF THE PLAN

Acquisition of Land

When was the notification for the acquisition of land published?

Under what Act was the notification for acquisition of land issued?

Please describe the process for acquisition of land: specifically, point out the legal difficulties faced; determination of compensation; method of payment for the compensation; duration of the acquisition process; etc.

125

When was the land finally acquired? If the entire land was not acquired at the same time, please indicate the amount of land acquired at each stage; time of its acquisition; purpose for which it was to be developed; and its location, etc.

Total compensation paid for the acquisition of land?

In what form and when was the compensation paid to the previous owners of the land?

Disposal of Land

What type of development/improvements were carried out before selling or leasing of land for different land uses?

By whom were these developments carried out?
    Public Agency-specify
    Private Contractor
    Any Other Arrangement - please describe

Was the entire land developed at the same time?   Yes/No

If the answer to the above question is in the negative, please give the time schedule for the development of land for different uses/different sectors.

Which organization/authority was responsible for effecting policies of land disposal?

Was the land leased or sold? If both the methods were used, please indicate for what specific uses the land was leased and for what land uses it was sold.

What method/formula was used for determining the price of land, for different land uses and in different locations?

If the land was leased, please indicate the lease-period.

How was the annual ground rent determined for the leased land?

Were any provisions made for periodic revision of lease charges? If yes, please describe the arrangements.

APPENDIX B

Planned New Towns in India Since Independence

Name	State	Original Purpose	Sponsoring Authority	1961 Population	Ultimate Population
1	2	3	4	5	6
			A. Refugee Towns		
Rajpura	Punjab	Refugee Rehabilitation	Government of India-Ministry of Relief and Rehabilitation (now transferred to Punjab Government)	16,714	60,000 (Later restricted to 16,000 due to scarcity of water)
Nilokheri	Punjab	-do-	-do-	8,035	16,000
Faridabad	Punjab	-do-	-do-	39,852	50,000
Tripuri	Punjab	-do-	-do-	n.a.	n.a.
Gandhi Dham	Gujrat	-do-	Rehabilitation Department, Government of Maharashtra (now Government of Gujrat)	26,514	250,000
Sardar Nagar	Gujrat	-do-	-do-	n.a.	30,000
Kubernagar	Gujrat	-do-	-do-	n.a.	30,000
Ulhasnagar	Maharashtra	-do-	Rehabilitation Department, Government of Maharashtra	107,760	200,000
Hastinapur	Uttar Pradesh	-do-	U. P. Government	n.a.	10,000 (Approximately)
Govindpur	Uttar Pradesh	-do-	-do-	n.a.	25,000 (Approximately)
Naini	Uttar Pradesh	-do-	-do-	n.a.	10,000 (Approximately)
Rudrapur	Uttar Pradesh	-do-	-do-	9,662	50,000
Govindnagar	Uttar Pradesh	-do-	-do-	n.a.	n.a.
Ashok Nagar	West Bengal	-do-	Government of West Bengal	38,250	60,000

APPENDIX B - Continued

1	2	3	4	5	6
B. Refugee Colonies or Model Towns					
Model Town,	Punjab	Refugee Rehabilitation	Punjab Government, Department of Rehabilitation	n.a.	n.a.
Jullundur	-do-	-do-	-do-	n.a.	n.a.
Ludhiana	-do-	-do-	-do-	n.a.	n.a.
Ambala	-do-	-do-	-do-	n.a.	n.a.
Hoshiarpur	-do-	-do-	-do-	n.a.	n.a.
Hissar	-do-	-do-	-do-	n.a.	n.a.
Karnal	-do-	-do-	-do-	n.a.	n.a.
Rohtak	-do-	-do-	-do-	n.a.	n.a.
Gurgaon	-do-	-do-	-do-	n.a.	n.a.
Khanna	-do-	-do-	-do-	n.a.	n.a.
Panipat	-do-	-do-	-do-	n.a.	n.a.
Sonepat	-do-	-do-	-do-	n.a.	n.a.
Rewari	-do-	-do-	-do-	n.a.	n.a.
Palwal	-do-	-do-	-do-	n.a.	n.a.
Jagadhari	-do-	-do-	-do-	n.a.	n.a.
Chembur Colony near Bombay	Maharashtra	-do-	Government of Maharashtra, Department of Rehabilitation	n.a.	15,000
Mulund near Bombay	-do-	-do-	-do-	n.a.	10,000
Gandhinagar (Valivade near Kolhapur)	-do-	-do-	-do-	n.a.	7,000
Pimpri near Poona	-do-	-do-	-do-		10,000
Various Colonies Delhi in and around Delhi	-do-	-do-	Government of India, Ministry of Refugee Rehabilitation	n.a.	150,000
C. Administrative Centers					
Chandigarh	Punjab	State Capital	Government of Punjab	89,321	500,000
Bhubneshwar	Orissa	-do-	Government of Orissa	38,211	n.a.
Gandhinagar	Gujrat	-do-	Government of Gujrat	n.a.	150,000

APPENDIX B - Continued

1	2	3	4	5	6
D. Industrial Towns					
Steel Towns					
Rourkela	Orissa	To accommodate company employees	Hindustan Steel Ltd., (under the Ministry of Steel and Heavy Eng., Government of India)	90,287	100,000
Durgapur	West Bengal	-do-	-do-	35,346	100,000
Bhilai Nagar	Madhya Pradesh	-do-	-do-	86,116	100,000
Bokaro	Bihar	-do-	-do-	n.a.	n.a.
Refinery Towns					
Barauni	Bihar	-do-	Barauni Refinery Project (under the Ministry of Petroleum and Chemicals, Government of India)	n.a.	10,000
Noonmati, Gauhati	Assam	-do-	Indian Refineries Ltd., (under the Ministry of Petroleum and Chemicals, Government of India)	n.a.	4,000 (Approximately)
Fertilizer Corporation Towns					
Sindri	Bihar	To accommodate company employees	Fertilizer Corporations of of India Ltd. (under the Ministry of Petroleum and Chemicals, Government of India)	41,315	30,000
F.C.I. Town at Gorakhpur	Uttar Pradesh	-do-	-do-	n.a.	6,000
Naya Nangal	Punjab	-do-	-do-	7,987	10,000
F.C.I. Colony at Chembur, Bombay	Maharashtra	-do-	-do-	n.a.	n.a.
F.C.I. Town at Namrup	Assam	-do-	-do-	2,000	10,000
F.C.I. Town at Durgapur	West Bengal	-do-	-do-	n.a.	n.a.

APPENDIX B - Continued

1	2	3	4	5	6
Other Industrial Towns					
Pimpri near Poona	Maharashtra	To accommodate company employees	Hindustan Antibiotics Ltd. (under the Ministry of Petroleum and Chemicals, Government of India)	5,000	6,000
Rishikesh	Uttar Pradesh	-do-	-do-	n.a.	n.a.
Jalahalli (Bangalore)	Mysore	-do-	Hindustan Machine Tools Ltd. (under the Ministry of Communications, Government of India)	13,376	n.a.
Dooravaninagar (Bangalore)	-do-	-do-	Ministry of Communications, Government of India	8,000	12,000 to 15,000
Hindustan Aircrafts Ltd. Town	-do-	-do-	-do-	28,362	n.a.
Nayveli	Madras	-do-	Neyveli Lignite Corporation Ltd. (under the Ministry of Steel and Heavy Engineering)	10,296	n.a.
Govindpura (Bhopal)	Madhya Pradesh	-do-	Heavy Electricals Ltd. (under Ministry of Steel and Heavy Engineering)	20,747	n.a.
Jagannathnagar (Hatia)	Bihar	-do-	Heavy Engineering Corporation, (under the Ministry of Steel and Heavy Engineering, Government of India)	n.a.	100,000
Durgapur Durgapur Coke Oven Plant Town	West Bengal	-do-	Government of West Bengal	6,350	n.a.
Oil and Natural Gas Commission (O.N.G.C.) Colony at Baroda	Gujrat	-do-	Oil and Natural Gas Commission (under the Ministry of Petroleum and Chemicals, Government of India)	n.a.	7,200
O.N.G.C. Colony at Ankleshwar	Gujrat	-do-	Oil and Natural Gas Commission (under the Ministry of Petroleum and Chemicals, Government of India)	n.a.	8,000

APPENDIX B - Continued

1	2	3	4	5	6
Other Industrial Towns-continued					
O.N.G.C. Colony at Cambay	Maharashtra	To accommodate company employees	Oil and Natural Gas Commission (under the Ministry of Petroleum and Chemicals Government of India)	n.a.	7,000
Rajhara Jharandalli (Mining Colony)	Madhya Pradesh	-do-	Hindustan Steel Ltd. (Bhilai Steel Plant- under the Ministry of Steel and Heavy Engineering, Government of India)	23,346	n.a.
E. Other New Towns					
Dandeli	Mysore	To develop plywood and other industries	Government of Mysore	14,454	50,000
Nangal	Punjab	To accommodate employees of Bhakra Nangal Project	Irrigation Department Government of Punjab	34,572	n.a.
Barapani	Assam	To house staff of State Electricity Board	State Electricity Board, Government of Assam	n.a.	n.a.
Naharkotia (or Naharkatiya)	-do-	To house company employees	Assam Oil Company	8,877	n.a.
Kailagarh	Uttar Pradesh	To house the employees of Ram Ganga Project	Irrigation Department, Government of Uttar Pradesh	n.a.	8,000
Nepanagar	West Bengal		Government of West Bengal	8,780	n.a.
Kalyani				5,000	60,000
				(Approximately)	

n.a. - not available

Source: Based on replies to a brief questionnaire sent to all the ministries of the Government of India and to the Town and County Planning Departments of all the State Governments; as well as various pamphlets published by the State and Central Governments.

Name of the New Town: Chandigarh - First Phase

Land Acquired (acres) -8, 586   Population Ultimately Planned-500, 000
Land Developed (acres)-5, 000   Population Planned for the
                                  Developed Land   -150, 000
                                  Number of Houses Built by
Density for Developed   the Development Agency   -   9, 710
   Land   -   30   (48, 550 persons)

| | Capital Costs | | |
Function/Item	Total-Rs. Millions	Per Capita Rs.	Per Acre Rs.
Land Development			
Land Acquisition	9. 3	19	1, 084
Survey of Land	0. 6	4	131
Site Preparation	--	--	--
Water Supply	26. 3	175	5, 258
Sewerage	18. 1	120	3, 613
Drainage	13. 2	88	2, 638
Electricity Distribution and			
Street Lighting	4. 4	29	872
Roads and Bridges	20. 4	136	4, 075
Landscaping and Horticulture	5. 3	35	1, 054
Temporary Works	--	--	--
Personnel and Audit	13. 2	88	2, 650
Maintenance During Construction	4. 3	29	855
Other Costs	12. 1	81	2, 420
Building Construction			
Residential Buildings	76. 3	1, 572	30, 521[a]
Non-Residential Buildings: Civic	32. 7	675	6, 553
Others	54. 1	1, 114	10, 814
Personnel and Audit	19. 5	130	3, 898
Other Costs	4. 3	89	860
Total	314. 1	4, 384	77, 296

[a] Total area under government housing is about 3, 500 acres, including their proportionate share of other land uses. The per acre cost has therefore been derived by dividing Rs. 76. 3 millions by 2, 500.

Name of the New Town: Bhilai - First Phase

Land Acquired (acres) - 19,784[a]   Population Ultimately Planned -100,000
Land Developed (acres)- 2,302   Population Planned for the
                                        Developed Land   - 60,000
                                      Number of Houses Built by the
Density for Developed   Development Agency   - 7,500
    Land   -   26   (37,500 persons)

Function/Item	Capital Costs		
	Total-Rs. Millions	Per Capita Rs.	Per Acre Rs.
Land Development			
Land Acquisition	11.5	115	581
Survey of Land	0.2	4	102
Site Preparation	0.5	8	195
Water Supply	8.2	136	3,555
Sewerage	5.1[b]	85[b]	2,227[b]
Drainage	--	--	--
Electricity Distribution and			
Street Lighting	6.0	100	2,602
Roads and Bridges	12.2	204	5,314
Landscaping and Horticulture	2.3	37	971
Temporary Works	--	--	--
Personnel and Audit	3.0	50	1,312
Maintenance During Construction	2.1	36	930
Other Costs	1.1	19	491
Building Construction			
Residential Buildings	90.6	2,416	39,362
Non-Residential Buildings: Civic	18.3	488	7,943
Others			
Personnel and Audit	6.7	112	2,907
Other Costs	--	--	--
Total	167.8	3,810	68,492

[a] Includes land for the Steel Plant. Area for the new town proper is about 5,000 acres.

[b] Includes drainage.

Name of the New Town: Rourkela - First Phase

Land Acquired (acres) - 10,000	Population Ultimately Planned-100,000	
Land Developed (acres)- 1,613	Population Planned for the Developed Land	- 60,000
	Number of Houses Built by	
Density for Developed	the Development Agency	- 7,500
Land - 37	(37,500 persons)	

	Capital Costs		
Function/Item	Total-Rs. Millions	Per Capita Rs.	Per Acre Rs.
Land Development			
Land Acquisition	8.4	84	840
Survey of Land	0.1	2	69
Site Preparation	--	--	--
Water Supply	10.3	172	6,409
Sewerage	8.3	139	5,174
Drainage	0.8	13	466
Electricity Distribution and			
Street Lighting	7.5	124	4,623
Roads and Bridges	7.0	116	4,328
Landscaping and Horticulture	0.7	12	440
Temporary Works	7.8	130	4,826
Personnel and Audit	3.2	53	1,963
Maintenance During Construction	3.7	62	2,294
Other Costs	2.6	43	1,612
Building Construction			
Residential Buildings	64.8	1,728	40,173
Non-Residential Buildings: Civic Others	12.0	320	7,438
Personnel and Audit	4.3	72	2,693
Other Costs	1.8	49	1,136
Total	143.3	3,119	84,484

Name of the New Town: Durgapur - First Phase

Land Acquired (acres) -10,462   Population Ultimately Planned-150,000
Land Developed (acres)- 2,700   Population Planned for the
                              Developed Land   - 70,000
                              Number of Houses Built by
Density for Developed   the Development Agency   -   7,500
   Land   -   26   (37,500 persons)

	Capital Costs		
Function/Item	Total-Rs. Millions	Per Capita Rs.	Per Acre Rs.
Land Development			
Land Acquisition	10.1	145	970
Survey of Land	0.1	2	53
Site Preparation	2.5	4	936
Water Supply	10.4	148	3,835
Sewerage	8.1	116	3,012
Drainage	2.0	29	741
Electricity Distribution and			
Street Lighting	9.2	131	3,399
Roads and Bridges	11.8	168	4,356
Landscaping and Horticulture	1.6	24	611
Temporary Works	6.4	92	2,389
Personnel and Audit	4.1	59	1,514
Maintenance During Construction	4.1	59	1,523
Other Costs	3.5	50	1,295
Building Construction			
Residential Buildings	83.9	2,229	31,065
Non-Residential Buildings: Civic	16.9	450	6,254
Others	4.1	109	1,518
Personnel and Audit	6.2	88	2,285
Other Costs	0.4	9	130
Total	185.4	3,912	65,886

Name of the New Town: Durgapur - Up to Second Phase

Land Acquired (acres) -10,515   Population Ultimately Planned-150,000
Land Developed (acres)- 3,700   Population Planned for the
                                  Developed Land   -100,000
                                  Number of Houses Built by
Density for Developed   the Development Agency   - 18,084
    Land   -   27   (90,420 persons)

Function/Item	Capital Costs		
	Total-Rs. Millions	Per Capita Rs.	Per Acre Rs.
Land Development			
Land Acquisition	10.3	104	985
Survey of Land	0.2	2	48
Site Preparation	3.5	35	953
Water Supply	21.3	213	5,755
Sewerage	13.8	138	3,723
Drainage	3.8	38	1,036
Electricity Distribution and			
Street Lighting	15.1	151	4,072
Roads and Bridges	18.9	189	5,099
Landscaping and Horticulture	2.8	28	762
Temporary Works	6.4	65	1,744
Personnel and Audit	6.1	62	1,662
Maintenance During Construction	4.1	41	1,112
Other Costs	3.5	35	945
Building Construction			
Residential Buildings	165.5	1,830	44,726
Non-Residential Buildings: Civic	27.3	302	7,382
Others	4.1	45	1,108
Personnel and Audit	11.8	117	3,168
Other Costs	0.4	4	95
Total	318.9	3,399	84,375

Name of the New Town: Pimpri

Land Acquired (acres) -100   Population Ultimately Planned-6,000
Land Developed (acres)-100   Population Planned for the
                            Developed Land   -5,000
                            Number of Houses Built by
Density for Developed   the Development Agency - 893
   Land   - 50   (4,465 persons)

| | Capital Costs | | |
Function/Item	Total-Rs. Millions	Per Capita Rs.	Per Acre Rs.
Land Development			
Land Acquisition	0.2	35	2,100
Survey of Land	Negligible	--	--
Site Preparation	--	--	--
Water Supply	0.3	59	2,950
Sewerage	0.2[a]	33[a]	1,650[a]
Drainage	--	--	--
Electricity Distribution and			
Street Lighting	--	--	--
Roads and Bridges	0.2	47	2,360
Landscaping and Horticulture	--	--	--
Temporary Works	--	--	--
Personnel and Audit	--	--	--
Maintenance During Construction	--	--	--
Other Costs	1.2	235	11,740
Building Construction			
Residential Buildings	7.6	1,704	76,090
Non-Residential Buildings: Civic	0.7	159	7,110
Others			
Personnel and Audit	--	--	--
Other Costs	0.4	80	3,590
Total	10.8	2,352	107,590

[a] Includes drainage.

Name of the New Town: Namrup

Land Acquired (acres) -809
Land Developed (acres)-417

Density for Developed
   Land   - 24

Population Ultimately Planned-10,000
Population Planned for the
   Developed Land   -10,000
Number of Houses Built by
   the Development Agency - 1,000
   (5,000 persons)

Function/Item	Capital Costs		
	Total-Rs. Millions	Per Capita Rs.	Per Acre Rs.
Land Development			
Land Acquisition	1.3	133	3,185
Survey of Land	--	--	--
Site Preparation	0.2	22	525
Water Supply	1.3	125	2,998
Sewerage	1.3[a]	134[a]	3,218[a]
Drainage	--	--	--
Electricity Distribution and			
Street Lighting	1.2	115	2,758
Roads and Bridges	0.6	57	1,374
Landscaping and Horticulture	--	--	--
Temporary Works	--	--	--
Personnel and Audit	--	--	--
Maintenance During Construction	--	--	--
Other Costs	0.2	19	446
Building Construction			
Residential Buildings	9.8	1,960	23,501
Non-Residential Buildings: Civic Others	1.6	322	3,856
Personnel and Audit	--	--	--
Other Costs	--	--	--
Total	17.5	2,887	41,861

[a] Includes drainage.

APPENDIX D

Calculation of Economic Rent for Different Categories of Government Housing

Name of the New Town: Chandigarh

Income Group Per Month	Construction Cost Rs.	Establishment Cost[a] Rs.	Total Construction Cost Rs. (2+3)	Plot Area S=ft.	Land Cost[b] Rs.	6 as % of 4	Land + Construction Cost Rs. (4+6)	Monthly Economic Rent at 8.5%	Monthly Economic Rent at 10%
1	2	3	4	5	6	7	8	9	10
Rs. 50-100	5,559	556	6,115	1,125	969	16	7,084	50	59
Rs. 101-175	9,800	980	10,780	1,125	969	9	11,749	83	98
Rs. 176-250	11,900	1,190	13,090	1,687	1,350	10	14,440	102	120
Rs. 251-500	17,650	1,765	19,415	2,250	1,800	9	21,215	150	177
Rs. 501-750	23,000	2,300	25,300	4,500	3,600	14	28,900	205	241
Rs. 751-1,000	29,000	2,900	31,900	9,000	7,200	23	39,100	277	326
Rs. 1,001-1,500	38,000	3,800	41,800	18,000	14,400	34	56,200	398	468
Rs. 1,501-2,000	46,400	4,640	51,040	27,450	21,960	43	73,000	517	608
Rs. 2,001-2,500	50,500	5,050	55,550	29,250	23,400	42	78,950	560	659
Special--over Rs. 2,500	99,541	9,954	109,495	53,400	42,720	39	152,215	1,078	1,268
Average	7,896	790	8,686	1,633	1,306	17	9,992	71	83

a. For construction only at 10% of construction cost.

b. @ Rs. 0.80 per square foot.

APPENDIX D - Continued

Calculation of Economic Rent for Different Categories of Government Housing

Name of the New Town: Rourkela--Up to Second Phase

Income Group Per Month	Construction Cost Rs.	Establishment Cost[a] Rs.	Total Construction Cost Rs. (2+3)	Plot Area S=ft.	Land Cost[b] Rs.	6 as % of 4	Land + Construction Cost Rs. (4+6)	Monthly Economic Rent	
1	2	3	4	5	6	7	8	at 8.5% 9	at 10% 10
Rs. 50-110	3,000	165	3,165	1,200	1,080	34	4,245	30	35
Rs. 111-200	4,748	261	5,009	2,400	2,160	43	7,169	51	60
Rs. 201-400	7,003	385	7,388	3,000	2,700	36	10,088	71	84
Rs. 401-850	15,437	849	16,286	6,000	5,400	33	21,686	154	181
Rs. 851-1,600	23,524	1,294	24,818	13,000	11,700	47	36,518	258	304
Rs. 1,601-2,500	34,109	1,876	35,985	20,000	18,000	50	53,985	383	450
Special--over Rs. 2,500	82,000	4,510	86,510	24,000	21,000	25	108,110	766	901
Average	6,620	364	6,984	2,800	2,520	36	9,504	67	79

a. For construction only at 5.5% of construction cost.

b. @ Rs. 0.90 per square foot.

Calculation of Economic Rent for Different Categories of Government Housing

Name of the New Town: Durgapur--Up to Second Phase

Income Group Per Month	Construction Cost Rs.	Establishment Cost[a] Rs.	Total Construction Cost Rs. (2+3)	Plot Area S=ft.	Land Cost[b] Rs.	6 as % of 4	Construction Cost Rs. (4+6)	Monthly Economic Rent at 8.5%	at 10%
1	2	3	4	5	6	7	8	9	10
Rs. 50-110	4,969	298	5,267	1,200	960	18	6,227	44	52
Rs. 111-200	7,675	461	8,136	2,400	1,920	24	10,056	71	84
Rs. 201-400	10,909	655	11,564	4,800	3,840	33	15,304	109	128
Rs. 401-850	15,577	935	16,512	8,000	6,400	39	22,912	162	191
Rs. 851-1,600	25,281	1,517	26,798	12,000	9,600	36	36,398	258	303
Rs. 1,601-2,500	51,104	3,066	54,170	20,000	16,000	30	70,170	497	585
Special--over Rs. 2,500	93,189	5,681	98,780	24,000	19,200	19	117,980	836	983
Average	9,151	549	9,700	3,405	2,724	28	12,424	88	104

a.   For construction at 6% of construction cost.

b.   @ Rs. 0.80 per square foot.

141

APPENDIX D - Continued

Calculation of Economic Rent for Different Categories of Government Housing

Name of the New Town: Naya Nangal

Income Group Per Month	Construction Cost Rs.	Establishment Cost [a] Rs.	Total Construction Cost Rs. (2+3)	Plot Area S=ft.	Land Cost [b] Rs.	6 as % of 4	Construction Cost Rs. (4+6)	Monthly Economic Rent	
1	2	3	4	5	6	7	8	at 8.5% 9	at 10% 10
Rs. 50-110	4,131	---	4,131	1,000	700	17	4,831	34	40
Rs. 111-200	7,700	---	7,700	2,000	1,400	18	9,100	65	76
Rs. 201-400	11,774	---	11,774	4,000	2,800	24	14,574	103	121
Rs. 401-850	17,500	---	17,500	8,000	5,600	32	23,100	164	193
Rs. 851-1,600	24,392	---	24,392	20,000	14,000	57	38,392	272	320
Rs. 1,601-2,500	31,055	---	31,055	26,000	18,200	59	49,255	349	410
Special--over Rs. 2500	36,675	---	36,675	28,000	19,600	53	56,275	399	469
Average	6,373	---	6,373	1,911	1,338	21	7,711	54	64

a. Included in 2.

b. @ Rs. 0.70 per square foot.

A SELECTED BIBLIOGRAPHY

Books and Articles

Alexander, P. C. Industrial Estates in India. Bombay: Asia Publishing House, 1963.

Babu, V. Vithal. Towards Planning: An Examination of Policies, Snags and Priorities in India. Delhi: Atma Ram, 1950.

Barfivala, Chunilal D. Hand Book of the Law of Land Acquisition. Bombay: The Local Self-Government Institute, 1957.

Basu, Durga Das. Commentary on Constitution of India. Third Edition. Calcutta: S. C. Sarkar and Sons Limited, 1955.

Bose, Ashish. "A Note on the Definition of 'Town' in the Indian Censuses: 1901-1961, " Indian Economic and Social History Review, Vol. 1, No. 3 (January-March, 1964), 1-11.
_____. Indian Economic and Social History Review, 9.

Brown, W. H., Jr., and C. E. Gilbert. Planning Municipal Investment. Philadelphia: University of Pennsylvania Press, 1961.

Chapin, F. Stuart, Jr. Urban Land Use Planning. New York: Harper and Brothers, 1957.
_____. Urban Land Use Planning. Urbana, Illinois: University of Illinois Press, 1965.

Chaudhuri, Sachin. "Centralization and the Alternate Forms of Decentralization: A Key Issue, " India's Urban Future. Edited by Roy Turner. Bombay: Oxford University Press, 1962, 213-239.

Harris, Britton. "Urbanization Policy In India, " Papers and Proceedings of the Regional Science Association, Vol. V (1959), 181-203.
_____. "Urban Centralization and Planned Development, " India's Urban Future. Edited by Roy Turner. Bombay: Oxford University Press, 1962, 261-276.

Hirschman, Albert O. The Strategy of Economic Development, New Haven: Yale University Press, 1964.

Indian Institute of Public Administration. The Organization of the Government of India. Bombay: Asia Publishing House, 1958.

International City Managers' Association. Municipal Finance Administration. Chicago: International City Managers' Association, 1962.

International Perspective Planning Team On Small Industries. Report on Development of Small-Scale Industries in India-- Prospects, Problems and Policies. Submitted to the Ministry of Commerce and Industries, Government of India, New Delhi: Ford Foundation, 1963.

Isard, Walter. Location and Space-Economy: A General Theory Relating to Industrial Location, Market Areas, Land Use, Trade and Urban Structure. New York: Technology Press of Massachusetts Institute of Technology and John Wiley and Sons, Inc., 1956.

_____, et. al. Methods of Regional Analysis: An Introduction to Regional Science. Cambridge: The M. I. T. Press, 1962.

Jakobsen, Leo and Ved Prakash. "Urbanization and Regional Planning," Urban Affairs Quarterly, Vol. II, No. 3 (March, 1967), 36-65.

Lamb, Beatrice Pitney. India A World in Transition, New York: Frederic Praeger, 1963.

Lewis, John P. Quiet Crisis in India. New York: Doubleday and Company, Inc., 1964.

Lincoln, John C. Ground Rent, Not Taxes: The National Source of Revenue for the Government. New York: Exposition Press, Inc., 1957.

Marathe, L. H. Lectures in Rating and Assessment. Bombay: The Local Self-Government Institute, 1957.

Moak, Lennox L., and Kathryn W. Killian. Capital Programming and Capital Budgeting. Chicago: Municipal Finance Officers Association of the United States and Canada, 1964.

National Council of Applied Economic Research. Population Projections of India 1951-76. New Delhi: 1960.

_____. Long Term Projections of Demand for and Supply of Selected Agricultural Commodities 1960-61 to 1975-76. New Delhi: 1962.

_____. Urban Income and Savings. New Delhi: 1962.

Neyveli Lignite Corporation. The Integrated Lignite Project. Neyveli: 1964.

Panikkar, K. M. The Foundations of New India. London: George Allen and Unwin Ltd., 1963.

Pant, Pitambar. "Urbanization and the Long-Range Strategy of Economic Development," India's Urban Future. Edited by Roy Turner. Bombay: Oxford University Press, 1962, 182-101.

Park, Richard L. "The Urban Challenge to Local and Stage Government: West Bengal, with Special Attention to Calcutta," India's Urban Future. Edited by Roy Turner. Bombay: Oxford University Press, 1962, 382-396.

Premi, M. K. "Reclassification of the 1951 Census Population into Rural and Urban Areas on the Basis of the 1961 Census Definition of Urban Areas," Indian Population Bulletin, No. II (August, 1961).

Queen's University Institute of Local Government. Single-Enterprise Communities in Canada. A Report to Central Mortgage and Housing Corporation. Kingston, Ontario: Queen's University, 1953.

Rao, V. K. R. V. "Rural Development and Urbanization," The Assam Tribune (January 5, 1964).

Ratcliff, Richard U. Real Estate Analysis. New York: McGraw-Hill Book Company, Inc., 1961.

Rawson, Mary. Property Taxation and Urban Development. Washington, D. C.: Urban Land Institute, 1961.

Reserve Bank of India Bulletin (February, 1965).

Robinson, Ira M. New Industrial Towns on Canada's Resource Frontier. Chicago: Department of Geography, University of Chicago, 1962.

Robock. "Strategics for Regional Economic Development." The Regional Science Association Papers, Vol. XVII (1966), 129-141.

Sah, J. P., and S. S. Dutta. "Economic Development and Spatial Planning in India," Ekistics, Vol. 23, No. 134 (January, 1967), 33-39.

Santhanam, S. Union-State Relations in India. New Delhi: The Indian Institute of Public Administration, 1960.

Seligman, Edwin. The Shifting and Incidence of Taxation. Fourth Edition. New York: Columbia University Press, 1921.

Shafi, S. Saeedush. New Towns the Answer to Urban Congestion--Future Pattern of Growth for Communities," The Statesman (Calcutta: September 22, 1964), 6.

Shah, K. T. National Planning Principles and Administration. National Planning Committee Series. New Delhi: 1948.

Singh, Tarlok. "Problems of Integrating Rural, Industrial, and Urban Development," India's Urban Future. Edited by Roy Turner. Bombay: Oxford University Press, 1962, 327-334.

Statesman. (Calcutta: March 16, 1964).

_____. (June 27, 1964).

Stein and Polk. A Master Plan for the Steel Township at Durgapur, West Bengal. New Delhi: (August, 1956).

Stockholm, City of, Town Planning Office. General Plan for Stockholm. Stockholm: 1952.

Sovani, N. V. Urbanization and Urban India. New York: Asia Publishing House, 1966.

Suquet-Bonnaud, A. "Introduction" to au numero special sur las villes nouvelle, Urbanisme, Vol. XXII (1953).

145

Swamy, V. S. "Some Aspects of Urban Population," Indian Population Bulletin, No. 11 (August, 1961).

Tangri, Shanti. "Urbanization, Political Stability, and Economic Growth," India's Urban Future. Edited by Roy Turner. Bombay: Oxford University Press, 1962, 192-212.

United Nations, Department of Economic and Social Affairs, Regional Seminar on Public Administration Problems of New and Rapidly Growing Towns in Asia, Held at New Delhi, December 14-21, 1960. New York: United Nations, 1962.

UNESCO Research Centre. Report on a Preliminary Inquiry on the Growth of Steel Towns in India--A Study on Problems of Urbanization. Calcutta: 1959.

Vagale, L. R. "Basic Issues in Planning of Small Urban Communities and Case Studies of a Few Towns in India," Journal of the Institute of Town Planners, Vols. 33-34, 12-18.

Viet, Jean. New Towns, A Selected Annotated Bibliography. Paris: UNESCO, 1960.

Weber, Adna Ferrin. The Growth of Cities in the Nineteenth Century. Ithaca, New York: Cornell University Press, Cornell Reprints in Urban Studies, 1964.

Webster, Donald H. Urban Planning and Municipal Public Policy. New York: Harper and Brothers, 1958.

White, Melvin I. "Long Range Forecasting and Fiscal Planning," Report of the New York State-New York City Fiscal Relations Committee. New York, 1956, 341-347.

White, Morton and Lucia. The Intellectual Versus the City. New York: The New American Library of World Literature, Inc., 1964.

Wurster, Catherine Bauer. "Urban Living Conditions, Overhead Costs, and the Development Pattern," India's Urban Future. Edited by Roy Turner. Bombay: Oxford University Press, 1962, 277-295.

Zipf, G. K. National Unity and Disunity. Bloomington, Indiana: The Principia Press, 1941.

_____. Human Behavior and Principle of Least Effort. Cambridge, Massachusetts: Addison-Wesley Press, 1949.

Reports and Government Memorandums

Government of Madhya Pradesh. Madhya Pradesh (Periphery) Control Act 1959.

Government of Orissa, Health (Local Self-Government) Department. Notification No. 6191-LSG, June 19, 1964.

Government of Punjab. The Punjab New Capital (Periphery) Control Act 1952.

_____. Capital Administration. New Revised Project Estimate of the New Capital of Punjab Chandigarh. Chandigarh: 1964.

Government of West Bengal. Kalyani: A Plan for a Garden City. Calcutta: West Bengal Government Press, 1958.

_____. Durgapur Development and Control of Building Operations Act.

_____. Calcutta Metropolitan Planning Organization. Preliminary Report on Existing Land Uses in the Calcutta Metropolitan District. Calcutta: 1964.

India (Republic). Land Acquisition Act, 1894. Act I of 1894.

_____. The Industrial Policy Statement. New Delhi: 1948.

_____. Report of the Local Finance Enquiry Committee. New Delhi: Government of India Press, 1951.

_____. Census of India, Paper No. 1 of 1962, Final Population Totals. New Delhi: Government of India Press, 1962.

_____. Accountant General, Posts and Telegraphs, Compilation of the Fundamental Rules Made by the Secretary of State in Council Under Section 96-B of the Government of India Act, Including Orders, etc., Issued by the Secretary of State, Government of India, Auditor General, etc., and the Supplementary Rules Made by the Governor General in Council Including Orders, etc. Third Edition. Simla: 1959.

_____, Comfort Survey Committee. Report on Low Cost Houses. New Delhi: National Buildings Organization, 1957.

_____, Committee on Plan Projects, Building Projects Team. Report on Industrial Townships. New Delhi: 1963.

_____, Ministry of Finance, Department of Economic Affairs, Report of the Taxation Enquiry Commission. New Delhi: Government of India Press, Vol. III, 1955.

_____, Ministry of Finance, Department of Economic Affairs. Indian Economic Statistics. New Delhi: 1963.

_____, Ministry of Finance, Department of Expenditure. Memorandum No. 1068/SF/60, March 23, 1960.

_____, Ministry of Finance, Department of Expenditure. Office Memorandum No. EL(11)-PC/60, August 4, 1960.

_____, Ministry of Finance, Department of Expenditure, Projects Coordination Division. Annual Report of the Working of Industrial and Commercial Undertakings of the Central Government for the Year 1962-63. New Delhi: 1964.

_____, Ministry of Finance, Works Branch. Office Memorandum No. 14(16)/60-W, August 29, 1963.

_____, Ministry of Health, Central Regional and Urban Planning Organization. "Some Aspects of Municipal Water Supply in a Few Cities and Towns of India," Annual Town and Country Planning Seminar, Madras, 1961, Paper No. 16.

_____, Ministry of Health. Proceedings of the Second Conference of State Ministers for Town and Country Planning. New Delhi: Manager of Publications, 1962.

_____, Ministry of Health. Order No. F.19-13/63-LSG. April 19, 1963.

_____, Ministry of Health. Report of the Committee on Land Policy. New Delhi: 1964.

_____, Ministry of Health, Town and Country Planning Organization. Note on Location and Planned Distribution of Industries. New Delhi: 1964.

_____, Planning Commission. The First Five Year Plan. New Delhi: Government of India Press, 1942.

_____, Planning Commission. The Second Five Year Plan. New Delhi: Government of India Press, 1956.

_____, Planning Commission. The Third Five Year Plan. New Delhi: Government of India Press, 1961.

_____, Planning Commission. Fourth Five Year Plan: A Draft Outline. New Delhi: Government of India Press, 1966.

U. S. Advisory Commission on Intergovernmental Relations. Measures of State and Local Fiscal Capacity and Effort. Washington, D.C.: 1962.

Unpublished Material

Harris, Britton. "Problems Related to Real Estate Taxes." Memorandum dated May 1, 1959 to Members of the Ford Foundation Team for Delhi Master Plan. Mimeo.

Hillhouse, A. M. "Chapter on Capital Budgeting." Ithaca, New York, Mimeo.

Jakobson, Leo. "Regional Planning for Urbanization in Eastern India, Improvement Programme for Metropolitan Calcutta: 1964-1971," Report No. 21b, Calcutta: Metropolitan Planning Organization, 1965.

Jones, Barclay Gibbs. "The Theory of Urban Economy--Origins and Development with Emphasis on Intraurban Distribution of Population and Economic Activity." Chapel Hill, North Carolina: University of North Carolina (1960), unpublished Ph. D. Dissertation.

Lele, Jayant Khanderao. "Role of Local Government in Rural Development." Ithaca, New York: Cornell University (1965), unpublished Ph. D. Dissertation.

Malhotra, V. P. "A Note on Chandigarh Capital Giving its History and Administrative Set Up." Chandigarh: undated, mimeo.

Sah, J. P., and Ved Prakash. "Grants-in-Aid. Financing the Plan Series. Preliminary Paper No. 2. New Delhi: Town Planning Organization, Ministry of Health, Government of India (1959), mimeo.

Vagale, L. R. "Population Trends in India and Their Implications in Town Planning, Housing and Urban Development." New Delhi: School of Planning and Architecture. A paper presented to the Asian Population Conference held at New Delhi in December, 1963.

23